A RIVER

THE THREAD THAT BINDS

BUD BEAMER

In memory of Todd Evans Beamer

A small mountain stream cascades its way east to contribute its crystal-clear waters to the Deschutes River. David V. Evans.

ISBN: 978-1-949735-80-2 (sc)
ISBN: 978-1-949735-02-4 (hc)
ISBN: 978-1-948928-78-6 (e)

Because of the dynamic nature of the Internet, any web addresses or links contained in
this book may have changed since publication and may no longer be valid. The views
expressed in this work are solely those of the author and do not necessarily reflect the views
of the publisher, and the publisher hereby disclaims any responsibility for them.

CONTENTS

SUCCESS

"HE HAS ACHIEVED SUCCESS WHO has lived well, laughed often and loved much; who has gained the respect of intelligent men and the love of little children; who has filled his niche and accomplished his task; who has left the world better than he found it, whether by an improved poppy, a perfect poem, or a rescued soul; who has never lacked appreciation of earth's beauty or failed to express it; who has always looked for the best in others and given the best he had; whose life was an inspiration; whose memory a benediction."

Bessie A. Stanley, 1905

Mecca: surrounded by hills of the High Desert and banked by lush foliage, the cold waters of the Deschutes River provide beauty and boundless recreation. David V. Evans.

INTRODUCTION

THIS IS A BOOK OF three parts. It was initially intended to just capture my experiences of fly-fishing the Deschutes River, an exceptional stream located in North Central Oregon. I, like many others, love to fish, and I love the natural world and being outdoors on the flowing water. To help others enjoy the experiences vicariously, I recorded some of the happenings in the form of poems. The poetry is not Keats, nor Frost, or even Emerson-like in nature, but primarily simple poetry-like stories, some rhyming, some not, of occurrences on the river.

I found, however, that many happenings in my life other than just the fly fishing have had their origins in flowing water, whether in the river, on the river, on the banks of the river, or even from the water of the river itself. The multitude of thoughts dancing through my head, as well as some very significant decisions that I have made, have been spawned at moments when my senses were enriched by the nature of the river experience.

The day after arriving in Oregon to start my internship in Portland, my former wife and I visited Central Oregon and spent the afternoon hiking the Deschutes River on the Warm Springs Indian Reservation. I had read of this world-renowned river in McClane's *New Standard Fishing Encyclope*dia when I learned that I would be interning in Oregon. Now, experiencing the river firsthand, it all seemed surreal. A cold, clear, emerald-colored river filled with blue ribbon trout and steelhead, located at the edge of the high desert, didn't compute in a mind exposed to the warm catfish streams of Iowa. I was mesmerized, and so started the process of abandoning the thought of returning to my home state. (In all fairness, I have since learned of cooler, respectable trout waters in Northeast Iowa.)

We remained here in Central Oregon. We raised our children here. We have fished and drifted the rivers, worked on the Indian reservation, become involved in the local community, and, thanks to many hours of work and moonlighting and a pension plan, purchased a ranch overlooking the river, as well as a cabin on the river itself.

We, like other families, have ridden the rollercoaster of life. One stabilizing factor has always been the river, a place to clear the mind and get restored.

There are, therefore, chapters that deal with things other than fishing. The commitments, the passions, the values, the relationships – most have been colored in some way by this natural-world medium. "The River," a song written by Garth Brooks and Victoria Shaw, is a metaphor for life as a river and will weave its way throughout this work.

Hopefully, more experiences worthy of poem material lie ahead – for all of us.

October 2014

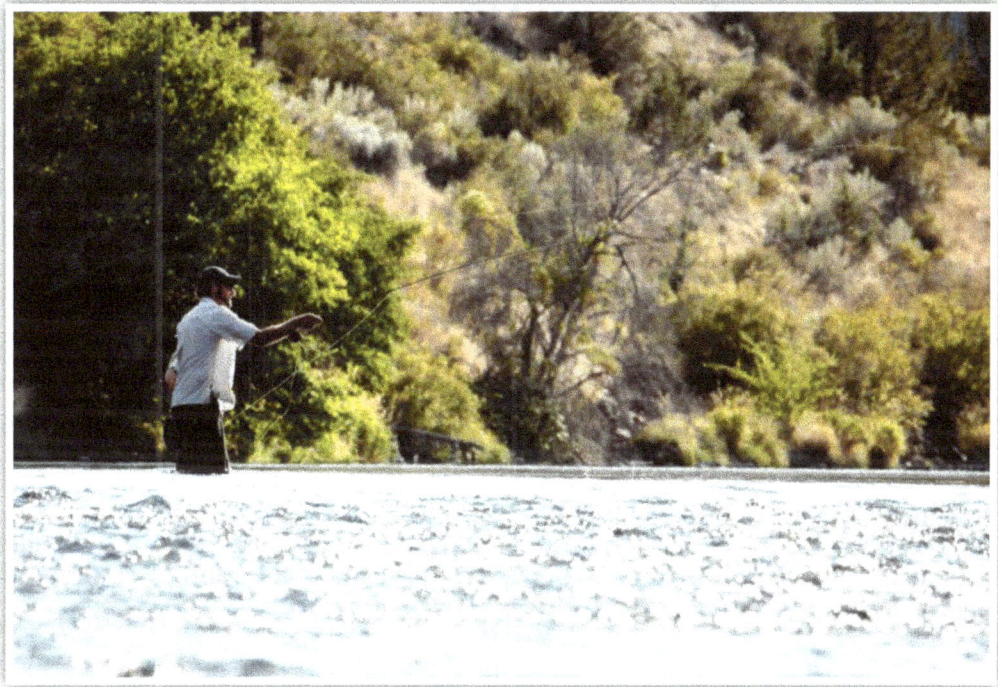

A casting fly fisherman. Casting a weightless fly effectively is an art that contributes to the overall satisfaction and rewards of fly fishing. David V. Evans.

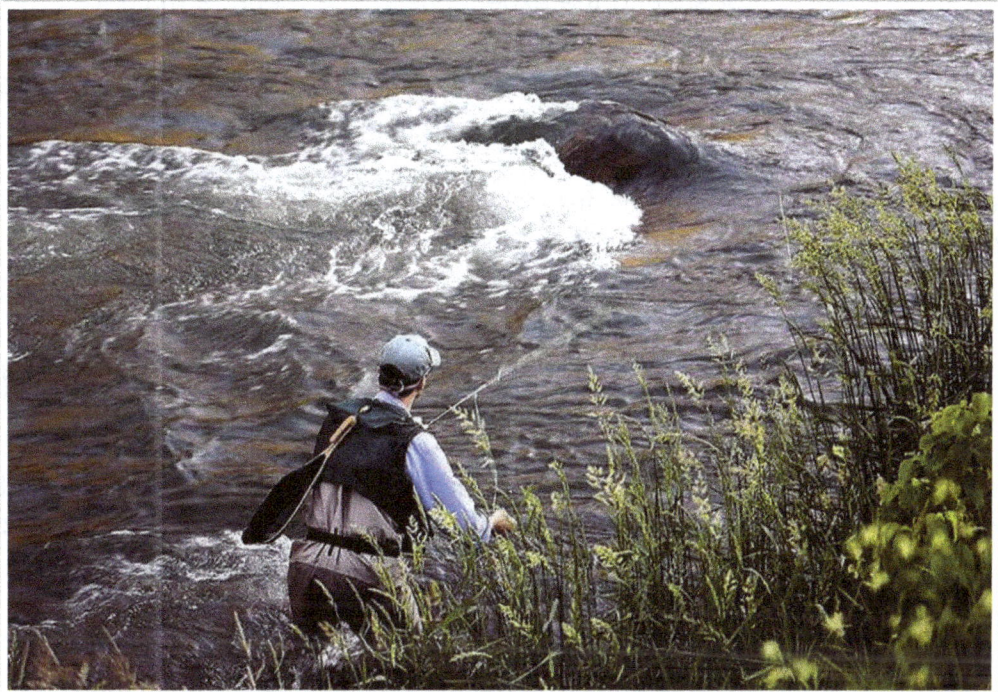

A fisherman stalks pocket water behind a boulder. Wading the bank is a challenge, but if a trout slip streams up and grabs your offering, it is worth the effort.

PART 1: FISHING FOR POEMS

I REMEMBER READING THE BOOK The River Why by David James Duncan and finding it remarkable that the central character attributed his passion for fishing to the fact that his mother had fished, somewhat excessively, while he was bobbing up and down in the womb.

I can relate to that phenomenon, for I too have a passion for fishing and I too had a mother who spent endless hours while she was pregnant fishing for bass, perch, and bullheads off of our dock in Iowa. She stated that she was so big she couldn't do much else, for she was carrying a set of twins. My theory weakens a little knowing that my womb-mate sister never fished a day in her life.

Still, I can't help but think that certain neurochemicals, released from the excitement of hooking and catching fish, passed across the placenta and stimulated receptors in my fetal brain that created an itch that needed scratching, a craving that needed a fix, as well as a pruning of my fishing inhibition centers. Something certainly set the fishing wheels in motion; the hook was set and passion ingrained.

Even though individuals may fish for different reasons, the love of fishing does seem to be intrinsic. Certainly, the joy of sharing the experience with a friend, a mate, or an offspring and creating memories overrides the importance of many things that we do with our time. The times spent in the natural world with the surroundings, the creatures, and sunrises and sunsets enjoyed in the comings and goings help complete each experience.

I'm sure that many of us have gone fishing when we should have been attending other responsibilities. I plead guilty on that count. There are also times when conditions are such that we should have stayed home. There are days that are so cold that ice clogs your ferrules and one fears the loss of body parts. There are also days that are so hot in the canyon that your corneas crinkle. The ambient temperature surrounding the river moderates the extremes – up to a point.

Also, personal trauma, incurred from a misdirected hook, being impaled on a broken branch, or crushing a kneecap after slipping on a "snot rock," redefines having "fun" fishing. As most know, hindsight and time always seem to mitigate the intensity of the displeasure. Take childbirth for instance.

Some adventures I forgot to remember. The better ones may be worth sharing.

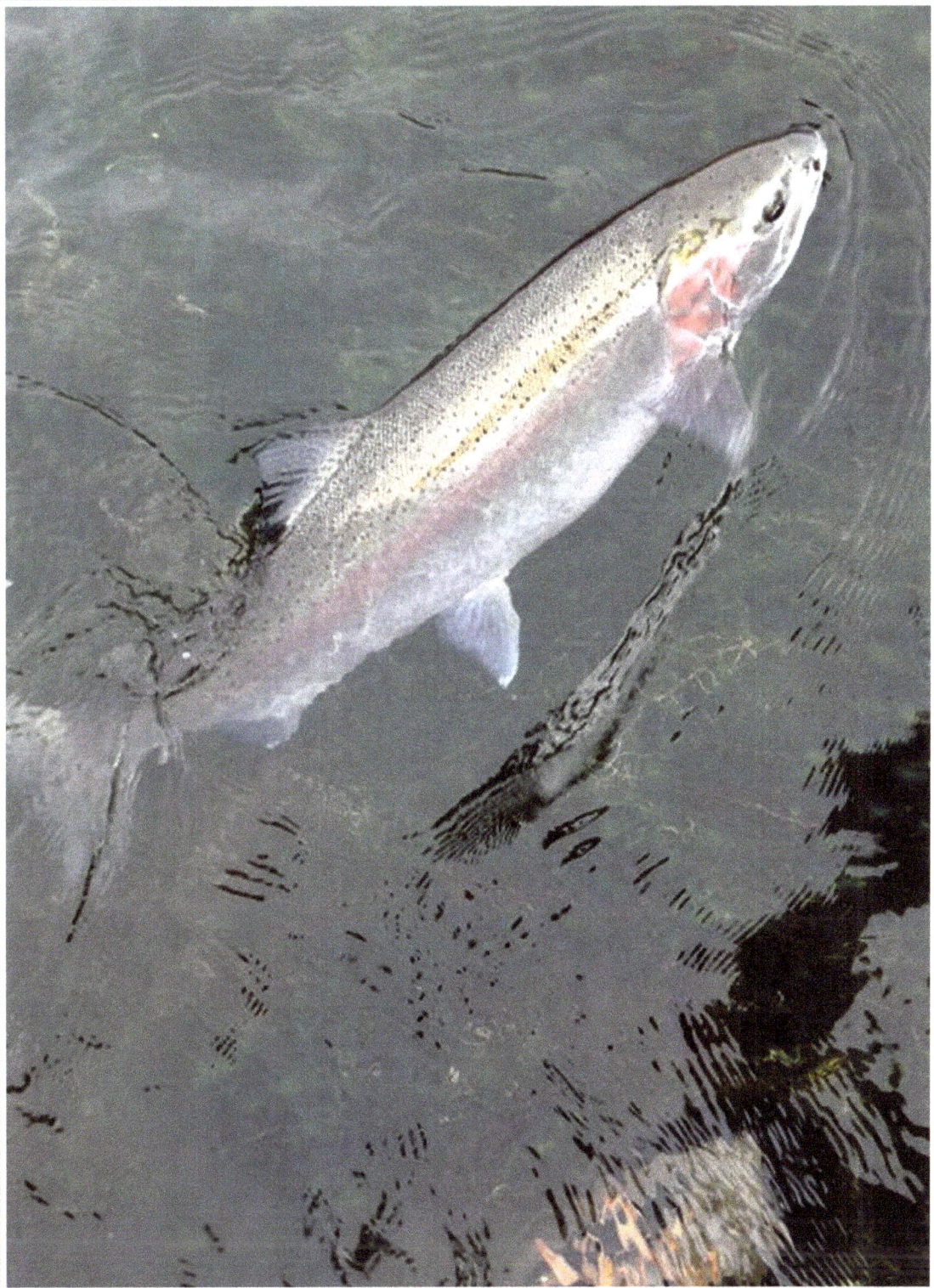

Fall Steelhead. The strength and beauty of this native steelhead matches the qualities of its natal stream, the Deschutes River. Author.

The Last Cast

It was the last day of the season,
the last light of the day;
one more cast and, reluctantly,
I'd pack my gear away.

The water swirled around me,
waist deep in the icy flow;
"one more cast," I muttered,
and then I'd have to go.

I lifted my line off the water,
my back-cast cleared the trees,
I eyed my prime spot through the fog,
and let my line fly free.

My fuzzy orange indicator
on a dead drift floated by,
my jet-black lead-eyed Wooly Bugger
poised on its final try.

I didn't need the indicator;
the great swirl let me know;
my arm jerked back to set the hook –
reflex from long ago.

Steelhead Falls. Winter steel heading has its own quiet beauty,
but conditions can "sting your nose and bite your toes" David V. Evans

The sudden strike caused a cry,
a sound no one would hear,
a response that's part of fly fishing,
like feathers, fur, and gear.

The first run was strong but short;
I held him in the pool.
If he made it to the rapids,
I knew he'd clean my spool.

I took a step downstream toward him,
a stalemate to relieve;
he sprinted for the rapids,
a place of no retrieve.

He cleared the water splendidly,
and then he leapt again,
a great steelhead flipped in the dark,
his splash an awesome din.

I stumbled, almost falling down,
as I tried to turn and follow,
my only hope to run with him
and find a place more shallow.

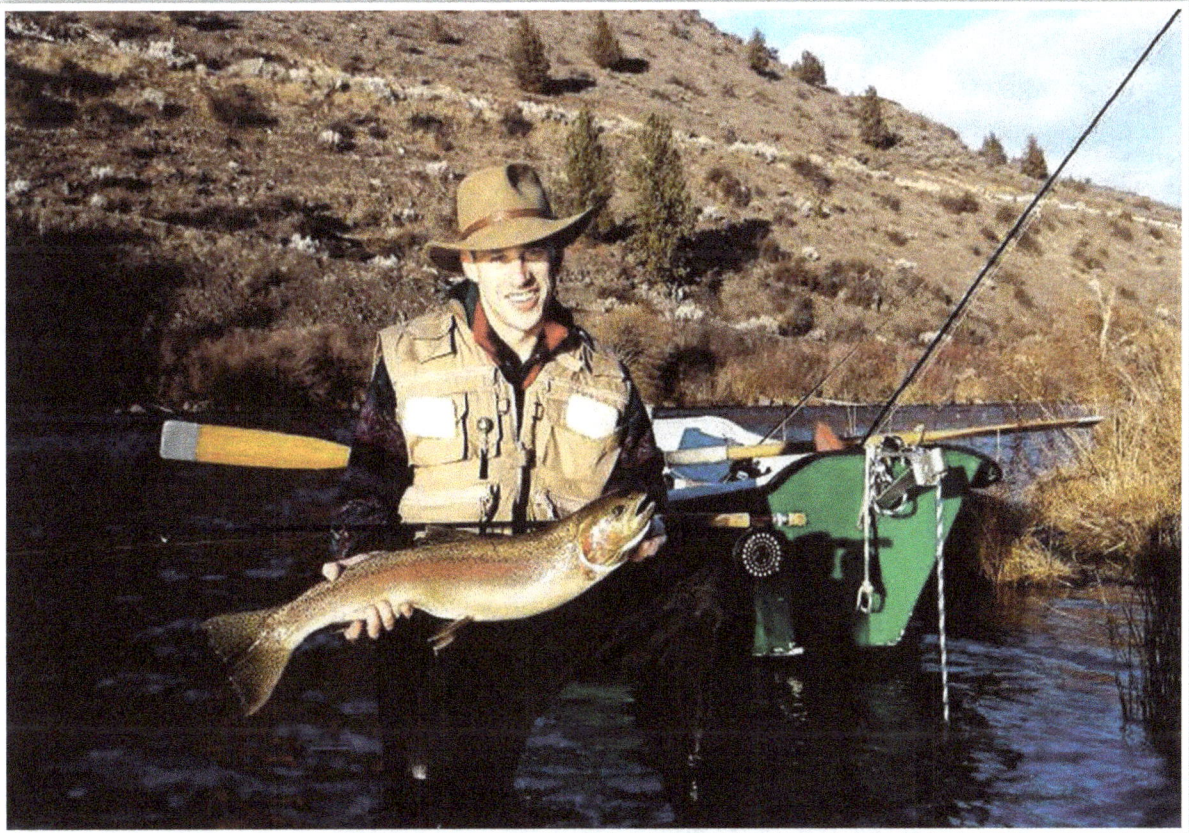

*Photographer, physician, fisherman, David V. Evans
shows off a late Fall Steelhead. Doug Williams.*

An eddy beckoned down the way,
a lighthouse in the storm;
I slid and slipped, held tightly on,
a footloose, awkward form.

A 3x tippet marginal
for a fish the size of this;
he ran at will, surged unrestrained –
for me 'twas total bliss.

The eddy pulled him to the right
but he came churning back,
my left hand working feverishly
to reel in all the slack.

And when he turned for waters deep,
sayonara came to mind,
but then the eddy's constant pull
was once again so kind.

Three more times this circuit course
he ran so gallantly,
my hopes would rise and then would fall
as he spurned the sight of me.

I was encouraged when he rolled,
but then he surged again.
I knew that hurried action now
would spell a dismal end.

So, carefully, I backed toward shore;
my six-weight felt the strain;
graphite was meant for times like this,
oblivious to pain.

He surfaced then, his white flag up,
presenting on his side,
I knelt and saw the fin was gone,
and lifted him with pride.

A hatchery fish, its tell-tale mark
an absence of a fin,
adds to the thrill – no native hurt
and food for twelve thrown in.

But even so I realized,
he'd fight no more again;
the double edge of victory
offset the thrill of win.

On New Year's Day, we bowed our heads
and I took a peek to see
a platter filled with sumptuous fish,
but more, the memory.

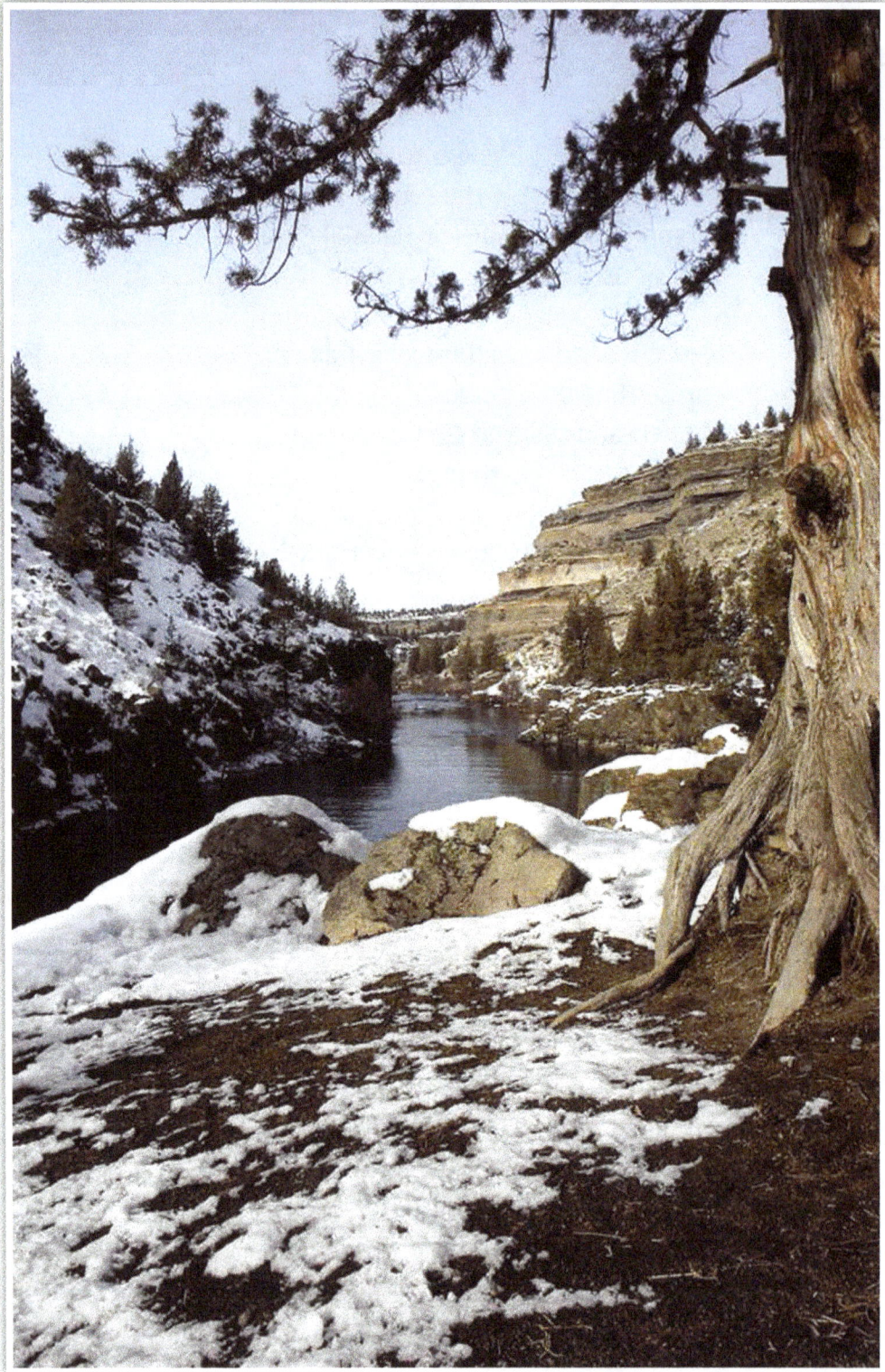

The innocent appearing Middle Deschutes silently carves its was through the lava layers. David V. Evans

A nice hen steelhead. A special treat on the last day of the season. Author

Two Types of Luck (Last Cast Part 2)

History often repeats itself.
Although situations are the same,
outcomes may be different.
Steelhead, for one, play a different game.

It was the last day of the season
and, again, the light was fading.
I'd been here thirty years before
in the icy water wading.

This time it was the Prince Nymph
that caught the Steelhead's eye.
I was shocked to see the bright, big fish
leap into the sky.

My drag was not as tight
as it apparently should have been.
I had released it just a little
when I reeled my last fish in.

It had thrashed around violently
when it got close to the shore.
My 3x tippet would have snapped
like it had in times before.

But now, I did not feel the hit
when he grabbed that small size fly,
And he was into my thirty-pound backing
before a blink of an eye.

I saw a fish across the river
leap then he leapt again.
It was my fish with most of my line
that had formed a mammoth bend.

He headed down stream and I followed suit,
my Last Cast poem in my mind.
Would this play out like the time before
when the outcome was so kind?

I was gaining on him as I stumbled along,
ecstatic and feeling alive.
The eddy was there, my confidence building,
but then my luck and I took a dive.

The current pushed me into a rock
that was the shape of a large pumpkin.
I fell head first into the river,
even my hat took a dunking.

The line became trapped beneath a rock
when my hands and rod hit the gravel.
The fish was still surging, the line pulsating,
but I sensed I was losing the battle.

I tried standing up but fell forward again
feeling the snap in my six weight.
I got to my feet, hand-gathered my line
but found my efforts too late.

He rose from the water a-dancing,
the line snapped as he flipped in mid-air.
He had survived the battle and season,
and had beaten me fair and square.

The eddy was there and helped once again
as I swam and crawled to the bank.
A snow drift was there that I slipped on,
another natural world prank.

I arrived at the cabin soaked and cold,
a little shocked at what had unfurled.
Despite a lost fish, broken rod, and dead phone,
I wouldn't have missed it for the world.

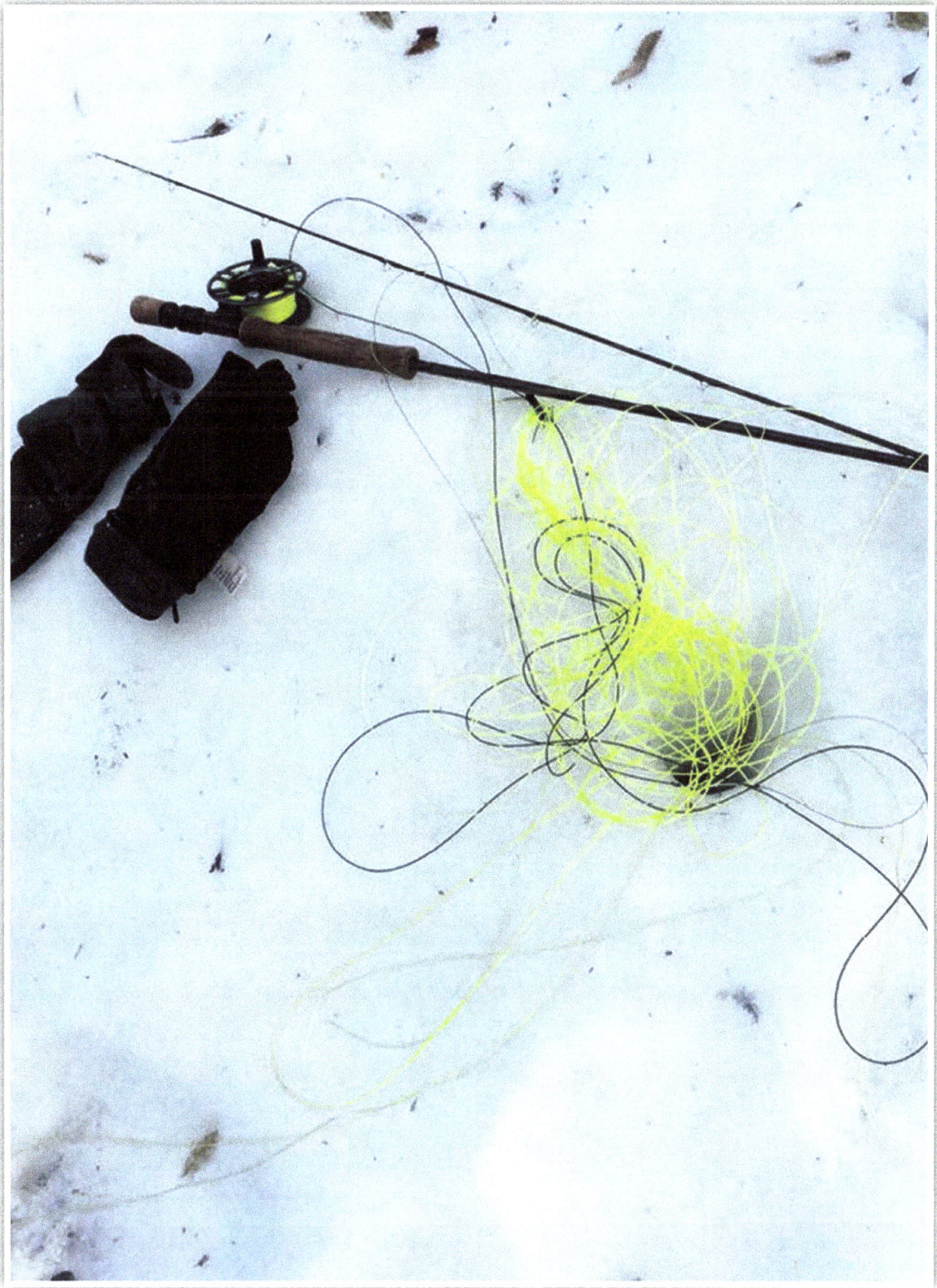

Broken rod, line, and backing: no sign of success here.

Some steelhead are easier to release than others. Jim Schollmeyer.

Fish on a Finger

The articulated leech is a prime example
of over-inventive minds.
Of effective function, there is no question,
outdoing most other kinds.

The double hook set up in marabou dressing
undulates, pulsates, excites.
The credulous steelhead, intrigued by this morsel,
puts it in high gear and bites.

There is that thrill of fish leaving water
and line being stripped from the reel;
the back-and-forth struggle of giving and taking
with that stout fish made of steel.

And then there's great hope as energy wanes
and luck escapes him but not me,
and I reach down delighted and, grasping the aft-hook,
twist in order to free.

A great transformation occurs in that moment
as quick as the blink of an eye.
As fore-hook impales me, the fish begins thrashing,
I'm no longer that calm, relaxed guy.

There's wailing and swearing and pleading and begging
as the fish brings me to my knees.
His strength has returned, he has renewed vigor,
he has taken the moment to seize.

A one-eighty rotation brings cold sweat and nausea
as the hook penetrates to the bone.
My life is in peril, I have to release him
from this digital pole of my own.

I try biting the leader that joins hooks together,
his head held in a death grip,
but realize suddenly that, pursuing this effort,
I'll soon have this fish on my lip.

My hand inches forward and, grasping the fore-hook,
I jerk and the battle does cease.
Hooks without barbs are endeared forever and ever,
a new meaning to catch and release.

The throbbing sensation gives way to reflection
as I stagger weak-kneed to the shore,
and I ponder the question that always will haunt me:
do fish feel the pain that I bore?

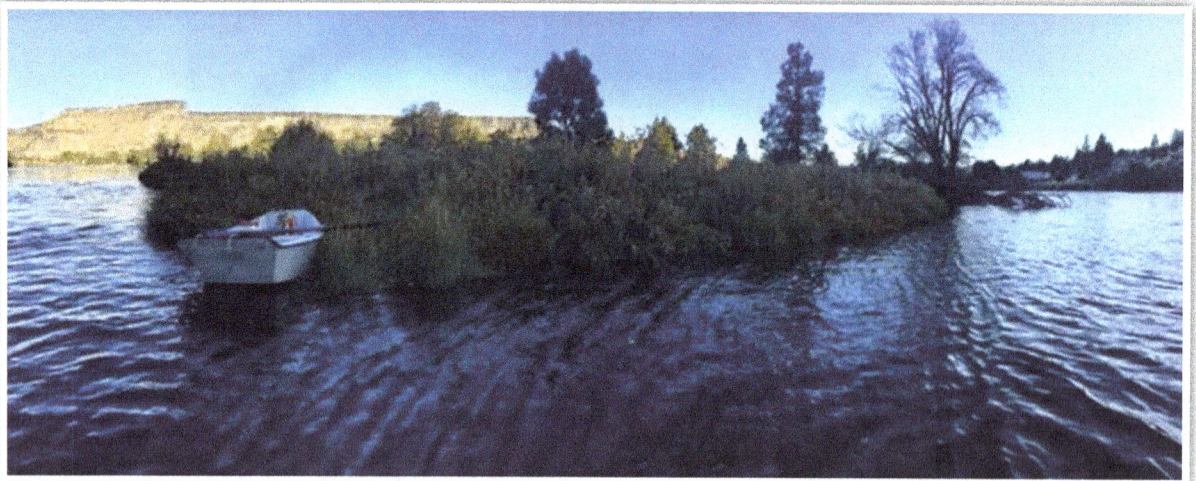

A beautiful place to hook a steelhead, on a rod or a finger. Abigail Beamer

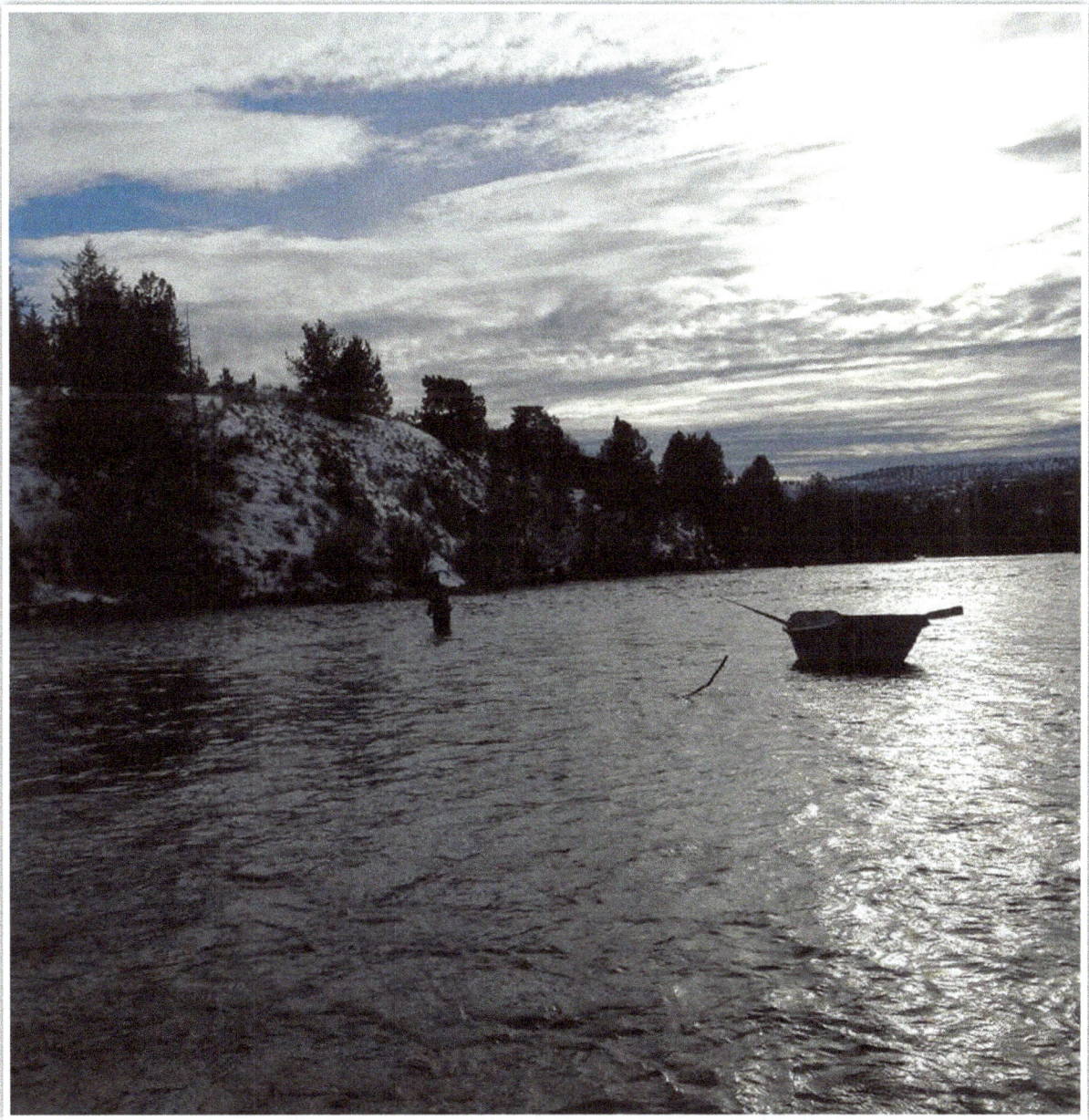

The fading light on winter's solstice adds a beauty of its own. Author.

Tight Connections

Preparing for a fly fishing drift down the river,
attention to a few details will save one some grief.
Peeing before putting on your waders is one prerequisite
and not missing eyelets with your line is certainly another.

These issues, however, are mere inconveniences.
Tight connections, however, will spare one major frustrations.
Many a fine trout or steelhead has escaped the net
as a knot untied, ferrules separated, or the reel left its seat.

Inattention to tight connections was the case one December afternoon.
We set out with the temperature low, but hopes were high.
New gear was assembled, in haste, I might add.
Cold fingers an accomplice in the unfolding chain of events.

A steelhead for supper had been the family request.
It seemed to justify leaving loved ones to go fishing.
The odds were against us with the snow and a brisk wind.
Not to mention that the bite was off and the river high.

Standing in the middle of the river, my legs became numb;
the rope to my Willy's drift boat tied firmly around my waist.
My partner upstream cried out "fish on", then shrieked again.
Something was wrong. His rod had separated at the ferrules.

A bright steelhead ripped downstream, leaping again and again.
"If the leader breaks, you'll lose your rod" I yell.
Then another yelp as his new reel falls into his hand.
It's quite a sight, him palming his reel, holding the stubby rod.

The steelhead, sensing chaos, gains strength and leaps and runs again.
The cold and darkening sky his allies as the battle wages on.
But there he is in front of me, his bright skin reflecting moonlight.
He flips and rolls, the leader holding as he thrashes defiantly.

As he makes another pass, I prepare for our "last ditch" effort.
With the cork rod handle clinched between my teeth,
my hands are free to sweep the fish into the boat.
He bounces once, flips in the air and lands in the stern.

We pile into the boat, disbelieving what just happened.
It seems surreal, but our hands and feet tell us that it's really real.
We laugh, fist bump, and then I mention the need to tighten connections.
His stare is as icy as the night air. "No admonitions – thank you very much".

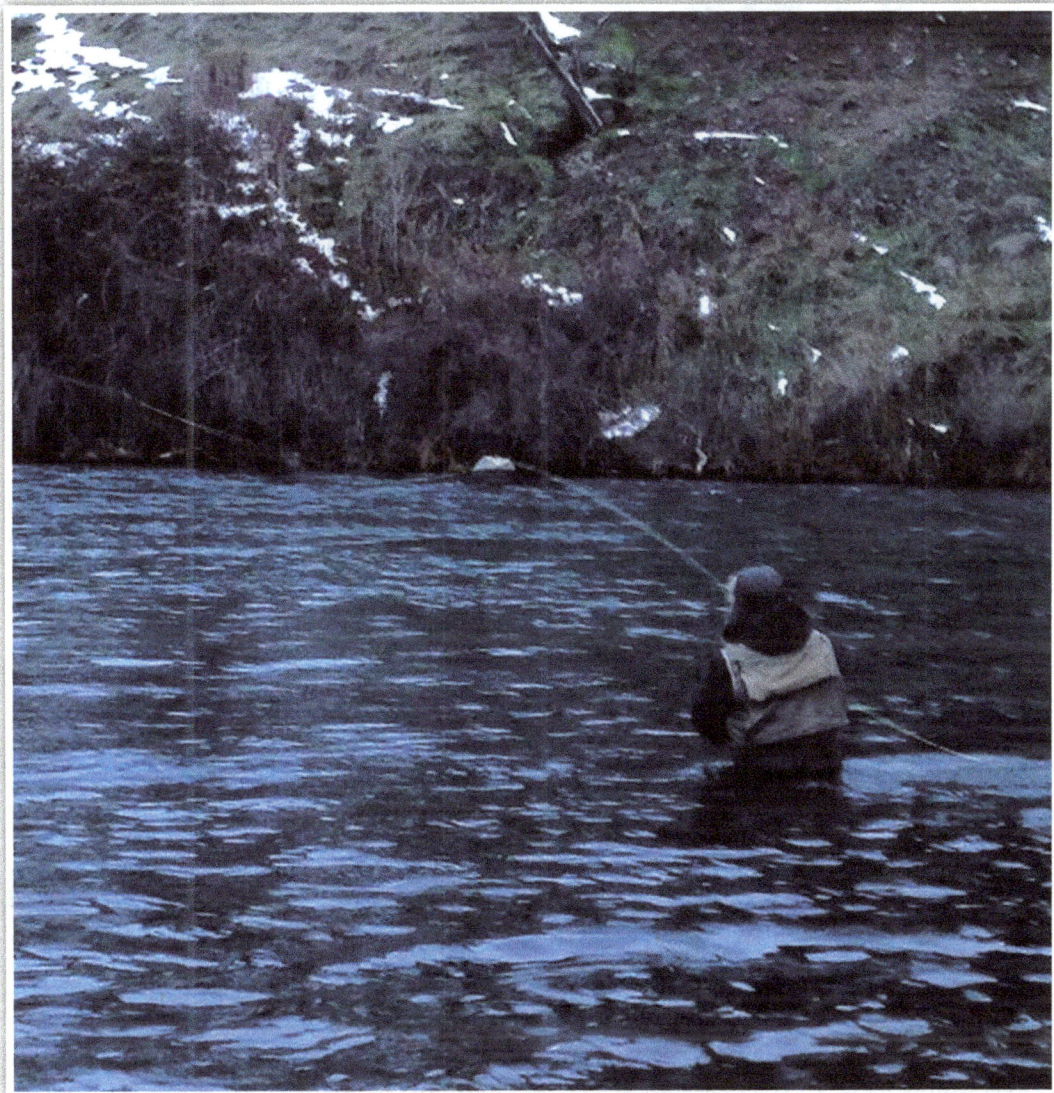

Darkness, cold, ice in the ferrules, and maybe even a fish. Author.

A Wheatley fly box holds Deschutes River Steelhead Flies—all potential "Hornets."
Clockwise from top: Green Butt Skunk, Turkey feathered Spey, Deschutes Flash, Max
Canyon, Purple Peril, Deschutes Deceiver, and in center, the Freight Train. Author.

The Nose Knows

It is a known fact that an embedded fish hook elicits pain.
The index finger has been tested and its owner pled for mercy.
Whether the lips of fish feel pain will remain a mystery.
But one thing is for certain: the nose knows pain.

My nose, for one, has been a recipient of a Green Butt Skunk.
A strong upstream wind had altered my cast's direction.
As the line moved forward, a searing pain shot up my nose.
Had a hornet chosen my right nostril to attack viciously?

The slack line bouncing in the wind made the attack relentless.
My hand found the assailant – my favorite fly had attacked me.
Cutting the leader removed the harness of the lively line.
The throbbing remained as I called for help from my upstream son.

Nobody intentionally wears a colorful fly as a nose ornament –
my son's thoughts as he approached, trying to act concerned.
"Don't touch!" I yelled as he reached to assess the impaled fly.
Even the slightest gust of wind caused fly movement and pain.

The trip could not end with this calamity, the fly needing extraction.
Nor would I consider a visit to the ER with this attractive piercing.
I had removed flies from faces, but not a #4 hook with a barb,
and certainly not from the bottom of the victim's nasal septum.

A loop around the fly's neck and a depressed shank set the stage.
Would the fly release or would a third nostril bless my face?
One, two, three and jerk. "Youch!" The fly left its perch.
My nose was intact, but a formidable hematoma ensued.

The swelling continued as we motored across the river.
Bozo the clown would have coveted my proboscis.
I changed to a Purple Peril and pinched down the barb,
proactive action in case the fly flew into my left nostril.

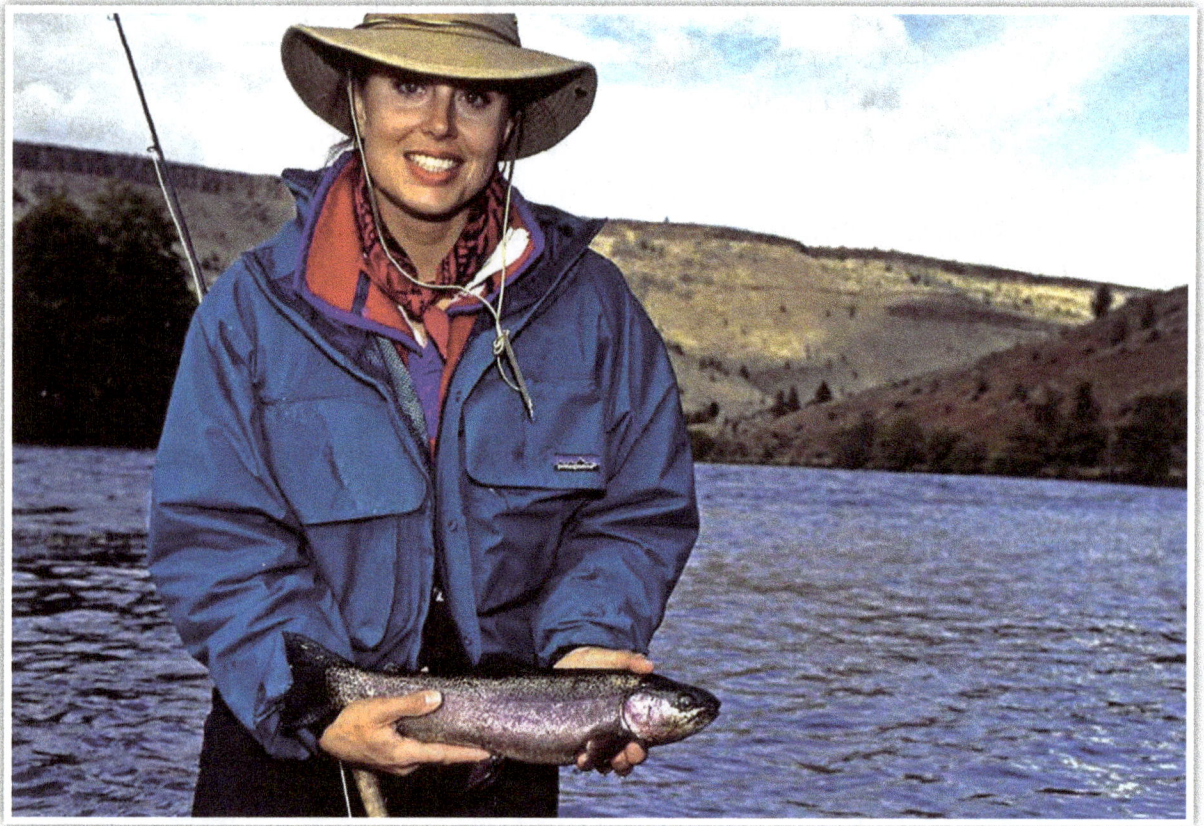

Beth Ann with trout: a much prettier nose and beautiful face, the rainbow was lucky to get a glimpse on its 10 seconds out of the water. Jim Schollmeyer.

To See Or Not to See

Sunscreen had blended with my sweat
as it found its way into my eyes.
My hat removed, I stuck my head underwater
and opened my eyes for relief.

My desire to fish the lower river had been
undaunted by triple-digit temperatures.
Maybe the intense heat would limit the competition.
So much for that theory.

The heat and now my blurry vision
brought my decision to fish into question.
Sunglasses, my new hat with its wet scarf drape,
couldn't keep the river's glare from my eyes.

I was reminded of a quarterback friend
who, in a pregame shower, got shampoo in his eyes.
The tearing and distorted vision were partially responsible
for five interceptions in "the game of the year."

He removed himself from the game,
longing to be anywhere but there.
He walked away from the cameras and post-game interview.
Seeing me, uttered "how's fishing?" as he walked by.

And here I was thinking that I'd rather be elsewhere,
perhaps playing football ... in a snowstorm.
My mind elsewhere, I stepped into a deep hole,
becoming buoyant and drifting downstream.

"Hey, you all right?" my partner inquired
as I drifted through his fishing "honey hole."
Swimming with my rod handle clinched in my teeth,
"Just cooling off," I stated unintelligibly.

He hooked a bright hatchery steelhead
moments after I had violated his spot.
I, naturally, took credit for an assist as I beached myself,
feeling invigorated and remarkably refreshed.

I emptied my waders, wrung out my socks,
and realized that my vision had cleared.
Two more hours of enjoyable fishing would take place;
no fish but an assist, in most sports, counts for something.

Chris Miller, quarterback for the St. Louis Rams in a critical game against the
San Francisco 49ers October 22, 1995. The Rams lost 44-10.
Chris never mentioned his visual issue publicly.

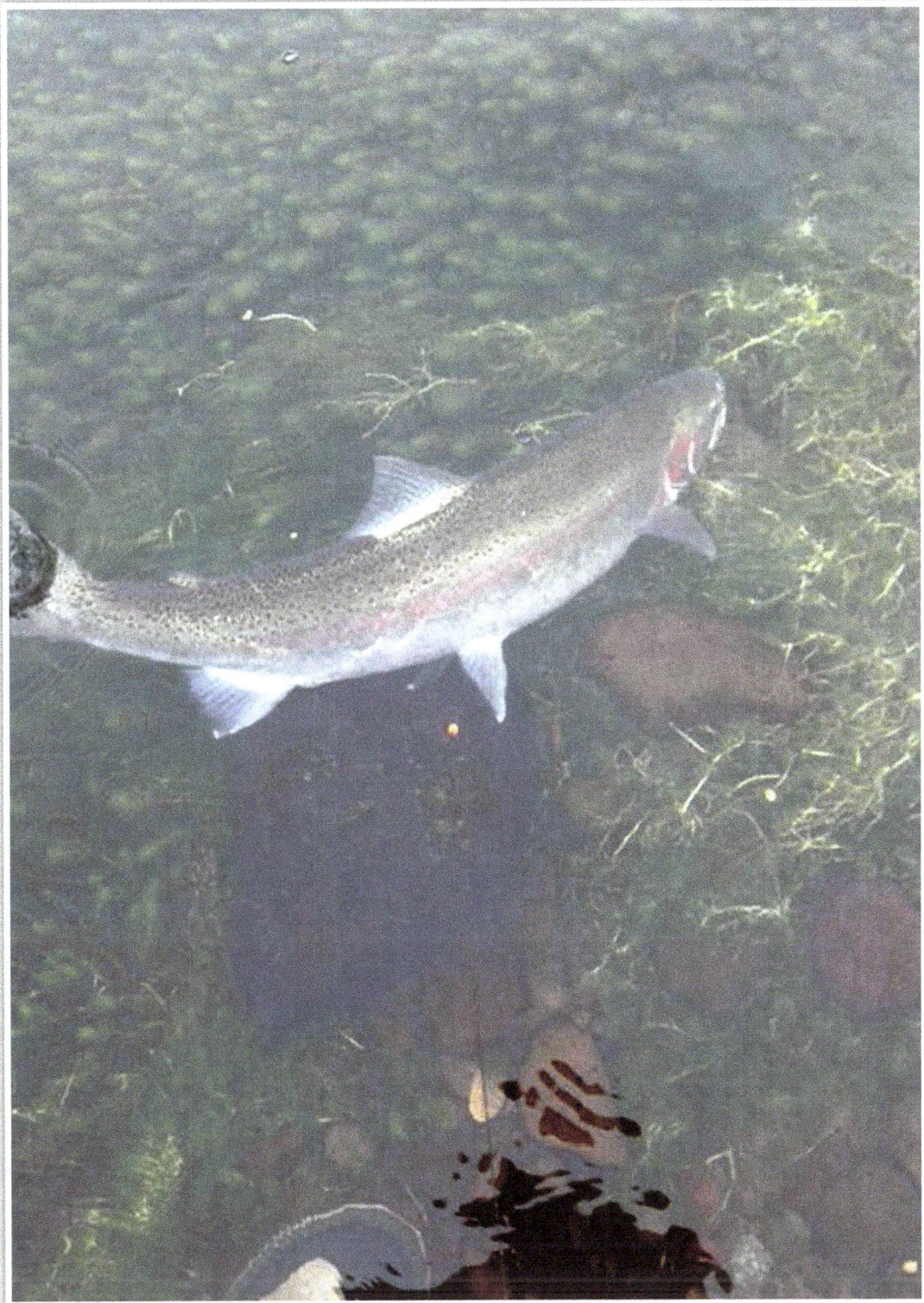

Steelhead. Fishermen can put up with some pretty adverse conditions if they can be rewarded with an epic battle and a fish the likes of this. Author.

*A fishing trip to the back woods of Alaska resulted
in this impressive looking King Salmon. Author.*

To Cast a Lie

Truth be told, it is honesty
that sustains a healthy relationship.
Lies, even little white ones,
can erode and diminish when revealed.

Some are proficient at deceiving,
criminals and politicians to name a few.
Even good people, like fishermen,
have been known to stretch the truth.

Embellishment, on some occasions,
may be necessary to enliven a tale.
Eyes widen with high numbers
or a lengthy distance between hands.

Pictures may seem to confirm the size
described in said fishing tale.
With fish in hands and arms extended,
the catch may become bigger than the catcher.

Deceit can come in many forms.
"Where did you catch those dandies?"
may demand a misleading response.
Who'd give away his favorite spot?

The "big fish" turned out to be not as big as was portrayed in first picture sent home to mother.

I did speak the truth on such an occasion
and sure enough there they were,
standing in our hole, with rods bent.
Oh, the look on my partner's face!

Beneath the big tree across from the Oasis;
our favorite Wednesday fishing spot.
The intruders are now there every time.
No way to take back the truth.

So, a twenty incher, a five pounder;
caught a dozen, lost a number;
estimating, rounding off, losing track.
Fishing stories, forgive the hyperbole.

Lengths, weights, numbers, places;
how accurate must one be?
In a noble sport, should honesty rule?
Are we noble or are we fishermen?
(Some are both)

Jordan and his companion Wirewest Kaptain ("Kap")
enjoying a day on the river. Artist Jane Rincon

A Fisherman's Best Friend

He stood by me faithfully,
not in the field but in the water,
waiting for that sudden rod set,
that "got em" or "fish on!"

His eyes fixed on the river,
looking for a swirl or splash.
He moved forward, becoming buoyant.
"Get back!" I ordered.

My retriever, born to retrieve
stuffed dummies and upland birds.
I treasured his companionship,
but fish and hooks, what a vexation!

My friend's favorite chocolate Lab
took off with a dangling lure.
Chaos ensued, with screaming and yelping,
the reel's drag emitting smoke.

Why deal with such calamities?
Dogs can be a pain at times
and a recipient of harsh words.
Leave at home. I think not!

"Ok, if I roll in this, my prey won't know it's me coming." Author

Retrieving is an innate quality.
Pleasing is also in a retriever's makeup.
Loyal, forgiving, a first-class greeter;
a lick, tail wagging – soul comfort.

Curled up in front of the fireplace,
tail thumping with your presence,
longing for a pat on the head
or a belly scratch – such ecstasy!

Taken for granted, perhaps,
but if departed, what a void.
Replaceable, conceivably, in time.
Don't expect your heart to understand.

So go roll in some putrid carcass,
eat my favorite running shoes,
knock my fish off my line,
but please, don't break my heart.

Fishing companion

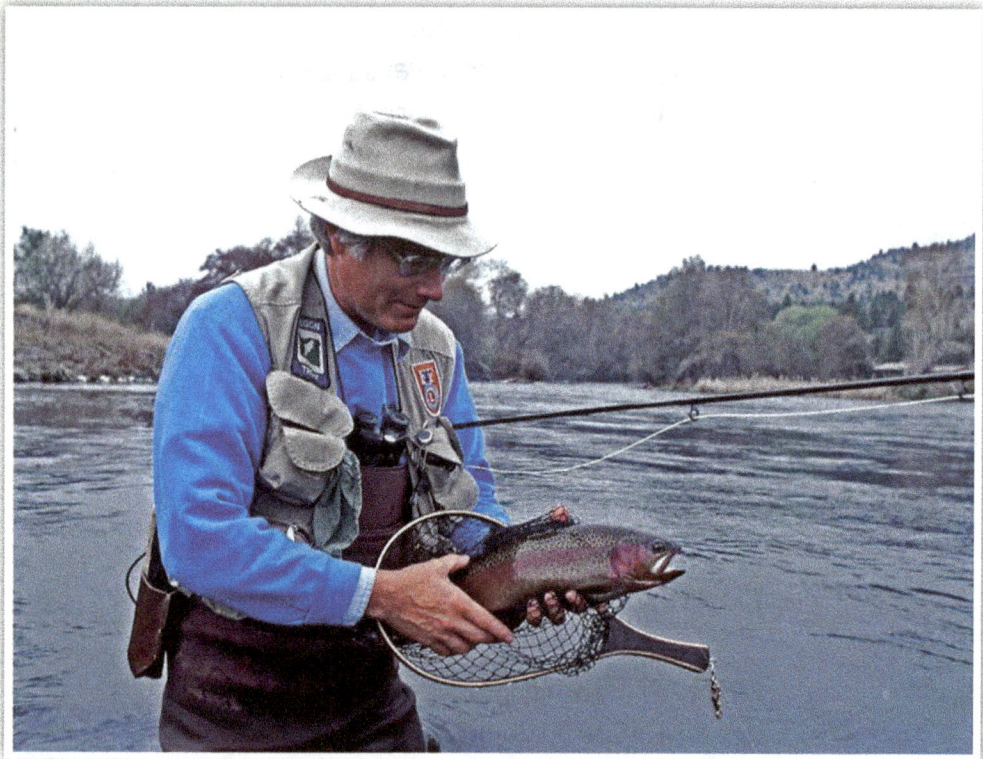

Dave Hughes with rainbow trout. Dave Hughes admires a fat native rainbow that mistook an artificial Blue Wing Olive for the real thing.

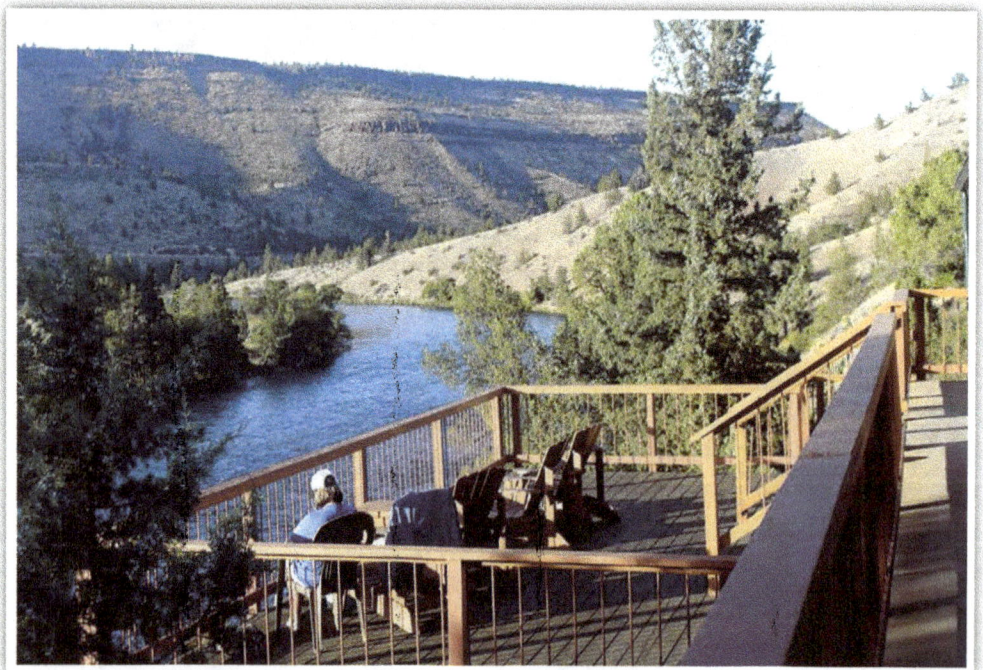

Redsides Deck. Relaxing on the deck at Redsides makes fishing a second priority.

HONOR WHEN HONOR IS DUE

THE NEXT TWO POEMS I have dedicated to Dave Hughes and three of his colleagues.

Dave's book, The Deschutes, has been appreciated and enjoyed by a multitude of fishermen and river lovers alike. Dave has been a most welcomed guest at Redsides Lodge, our fishing cabin on the Deschutes River, sharing many stories and plying the waters in front of the cabin, using his deft technical skills. We have fished together a few times, and the poem "Poetic Justice" reflects one of those experiences. He wrote an article in Flyfishing about that particular outing and in the article described the explosiveness of a big brown trout taking an elk hair fly. He compared it to an incident one night in Viet Nam when he sent a live hand grenade down-stream on a lily pad to a Viet Cong encampment several yards below. The detonation rocked the night. His writings are always vivid and descriptive.

In addition to Dave, we have also had the pleasure of the company of Jim Schollmeyer, Ted Leeson, and Rick Haefle. These fine gentlemen have contributed so much to the art and pastime of fly fishing with their writings, photography, fly tying, and entomology work. Their work is profound, as will be their legacy.

"Rebirth On the River" is an attempt to honor the four of them and give a sense of what fly fishing means to those of us who value this natural-world experience.

The professor of fly fishing writing and technical skills,
Ted Leeson, respecting the spirit of his early morning catch.

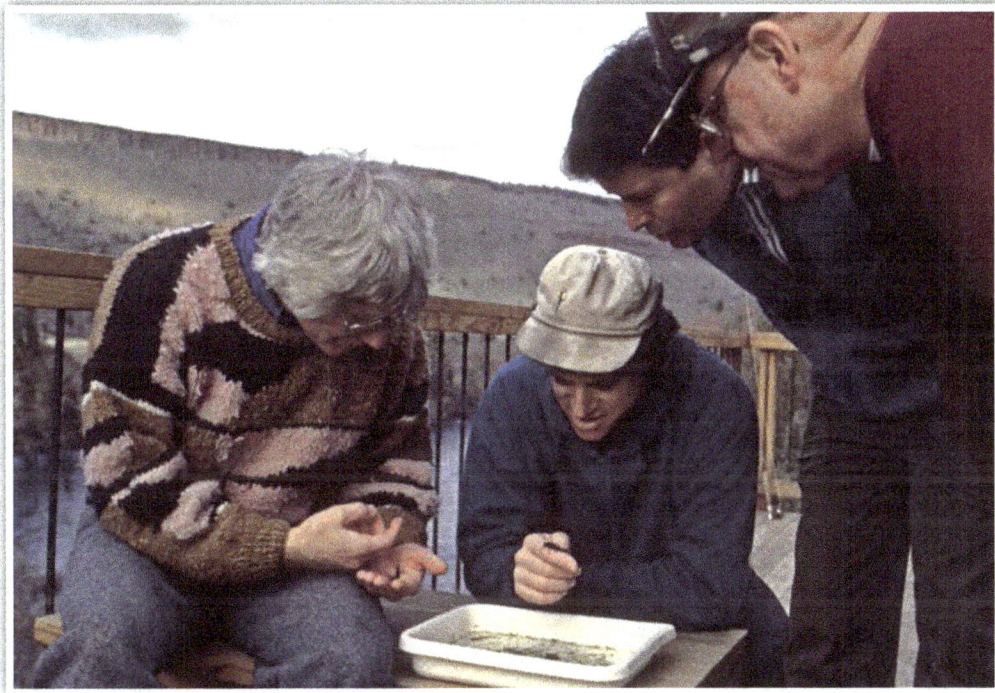

Dave Hughes and entomologist Rick Haefle discuss the early forms of "river bugs" with author and Dar Isenee. Jim Schollmeyer.

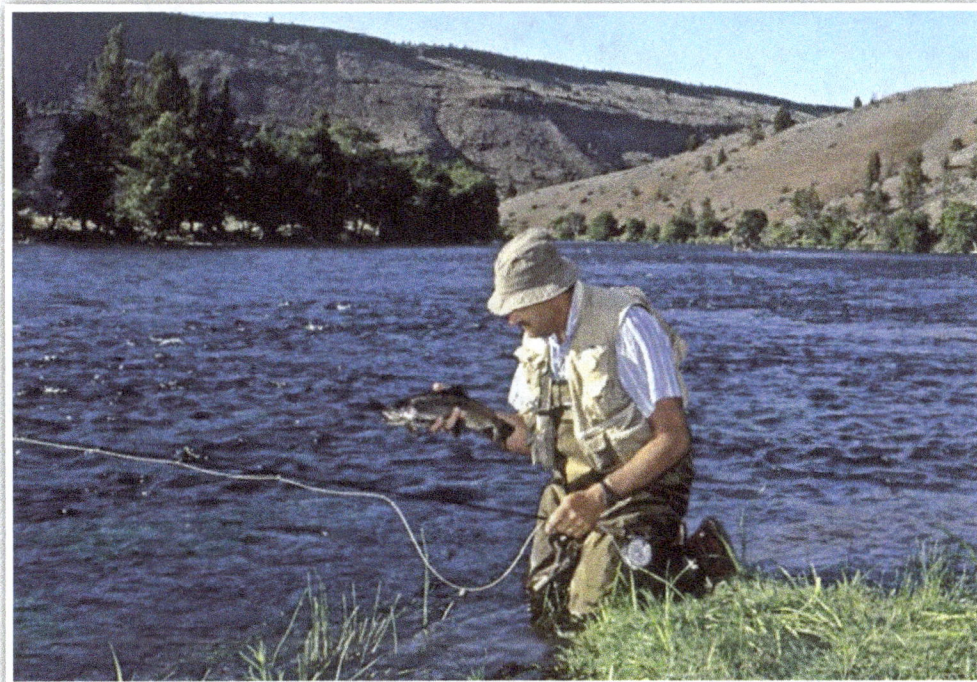

Jim Schollmeyer, noted author and photographer, doing what he loves and shares with others.

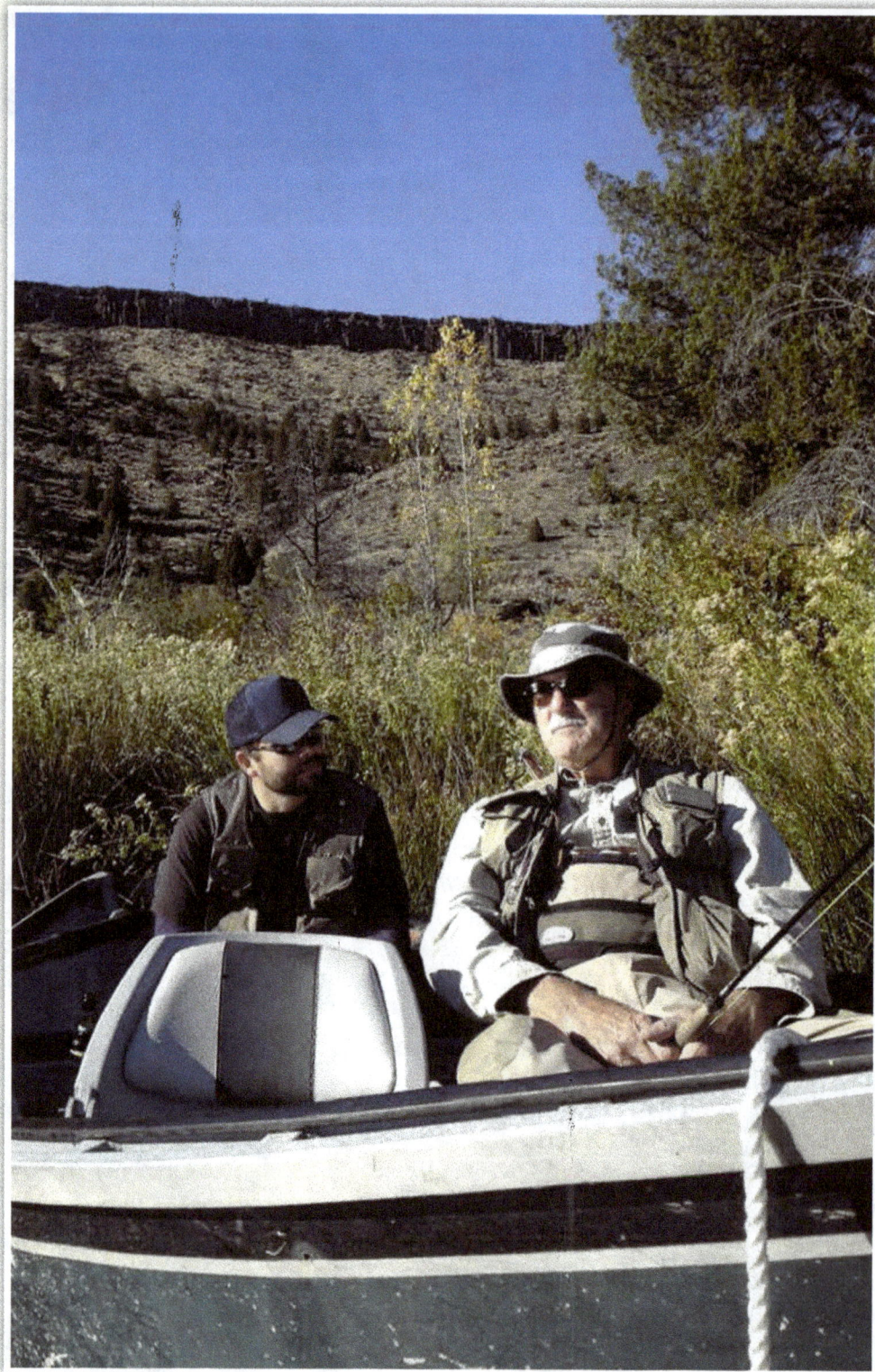

Jim Schollmeyer and Jordan. Jim offers Jordan Beamer sage advice as he and Jordan enjoy the comfort created by moving water and the dramatic surroundings. Author.

Poetic Justice

The hatch was not like yesterday's,
when mayflies filled the air.
But ephemerella lookalikes
were still the bill of fare.

Comparaduns and hairwing duns
'bout sixteen, eighteen size,
little olives, pale morning duns,
my fly box did comprise.

No matter that the salmon fly
still was on the wing
and a tied-down caddis or bucktail pattern
would excitement bring.

One felt compelled to match the hatch
of something near and dear,
no matter that my sidekick yelled
the oft-heard "fish on" cheer.

His bushy flies brought bended rod
and a smile upon his face.
My dainty flies of yellow or green
brought pride, tradition, grace.

A female Salmon Fly rests before ova positing her eggs, unaware that she and her like create one of the greatest of hatches and exciting experiences for fly fishermen. David V. Evans

A big rise beneath a tree
snuffed a big fly's flutter.
My partner offed me his rod
but I shook my head and muttered.

His elk hair fly, a behemoth thing
over the lair did fly;
amazing that it flew at all,
the friction quotient high.

The size four pattern's descent began,
perceived as the right brand,
no matter that the gullet was full,
the fish, a selective gourmand.

He hit it hard and took it down,
no leaps or acrobatics.
The run was long and deep and strong,
a true excitement fix.

I took it well – at least I tried,
not good as a spectator.
I had played the role the whole damn day,
a real irritator.

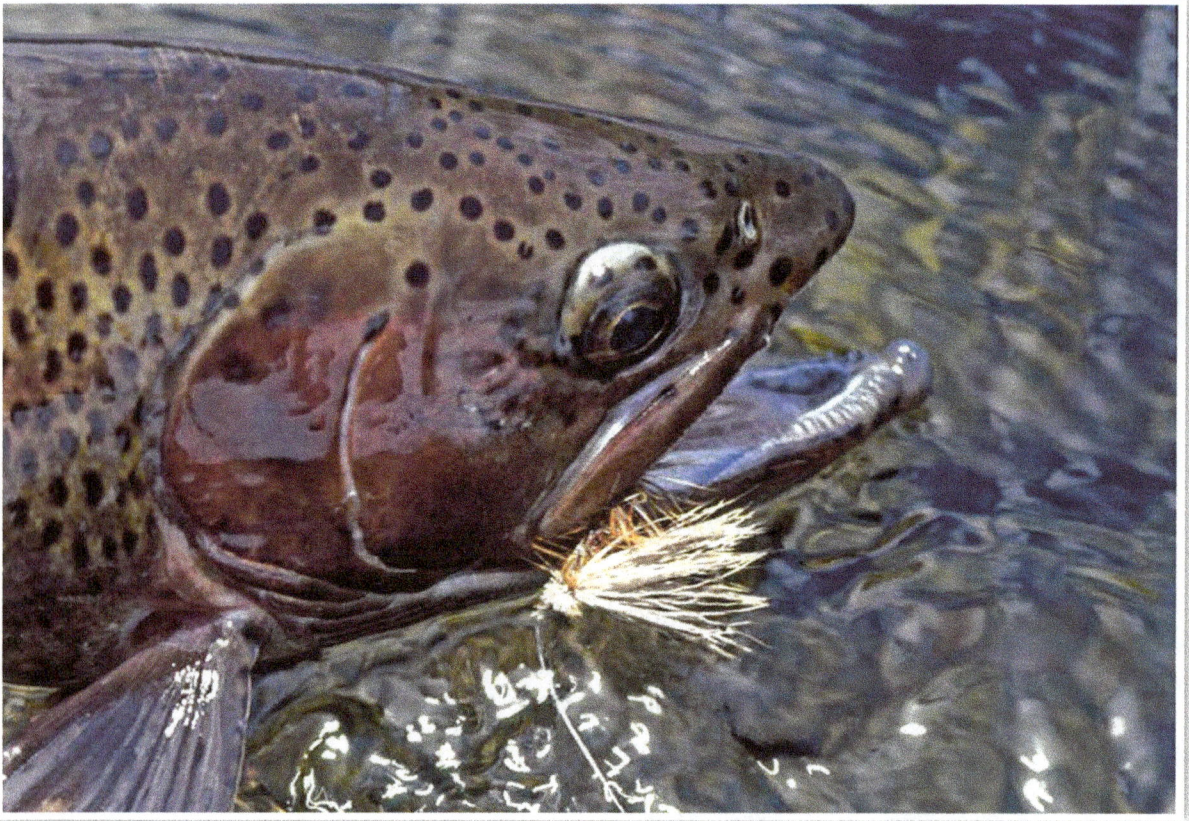

Rainbow Trout: bug-eyed but beautiful, a native rainbow with a Buck Tail Caddis that looked so much like a Salmon Fly. Jim Schollmeyer.

The big brown with flanks of gold
had been a pleasant surprise.
So I changed my gear and prepared myself
as I saw a big fish rise.

Enough was enough and, anyway,
there'd be more mayfly hatches.
Why carry a cause to its extreme
and miss the best of catches?

He suggested I come downstream by him
and get in a better position.
I stood my ground – I knew how to cast;
I wasn't about to listen.

My cast was slow as I paused to wait
for the back cast to unfurl.
The bulky fly plodded through the air,
awaiting to be hurled.

A dozen times I repeated this act,
wondering why I'd failed.
With an extra effort, I reached a snag
on which it became impaled.

*Dave Hughes releases a Brown Trout, an infrequent visitor
to the lower Deschutes. Jim Schollmeyer.*

The fly broke off because of the jerk
that was at the end of the line
and eventually fell as gravity won
as the snag released its find.

We both held our breath and watched silently
as the fly proceeded downstream,
and collectively gasped as a mouth opened wide
and inhaled away my dream.

I muttered some words that my friend barely heard;
he asked, but they weren't worth repeating.
It was a personal thing at the end of the day
when my ego had taken a beating.

It's like the fly and the fish somehow had known
that they'd been my second choice.
I had paid my dues; justice was served,
denied by pride to rejoice.

*Trout Creek. Moving water, a shimmer of light, maybe a fish
or two—an ultimate tonic. Jim Schollmeyer.*

Rebirth on the River

I needed the feel of a river.
I have a favorite or two.
The stress had slowly been building,
a fishing trip long overdue.

The discouraging daily headlines,
the pressure of everyday life,
demanded a panacea,
a place with limited strife.

Even my favorite pastime,
in a setting remarkably pure,
has given me anxious moments,
tricks played by Mother Nature.

Becoming adrift in cold water
or a rattlesnake buzz in the brush,
can get the old ticker a-racing,
a real adrenalin rush.

But fear in an out-of-door setting
can actually do one some good,
a tonic that cleanses the spirit,
restores as no medicine could.

The author's wife, Beth Ann, on what would have been Todd's twenty-ninth birthday, 9/11/97, with a rainbow standing watch. North Umpqua River. Author.

In contrast, the fear that's created
by society's ills and mayhem,
can deaden the soul and the spirit
and headaches and heartburn begin.

So give me my fly rod and river,
which will lighten the load in my heart,
where I can feel the water engulf me
and the knot in my stomach depart.

The shimmer of light on the water,
a beautiful sight to behold;
its calming effect as it glistens and gleams
is worth more than silver and gold.

Insects and man emerge in this light,
transformed as the process unfolds.
A new man rises, renewed and restored,
who can cope with what life now holds.

Reflection of sunlight on water. The calming waters. Author.

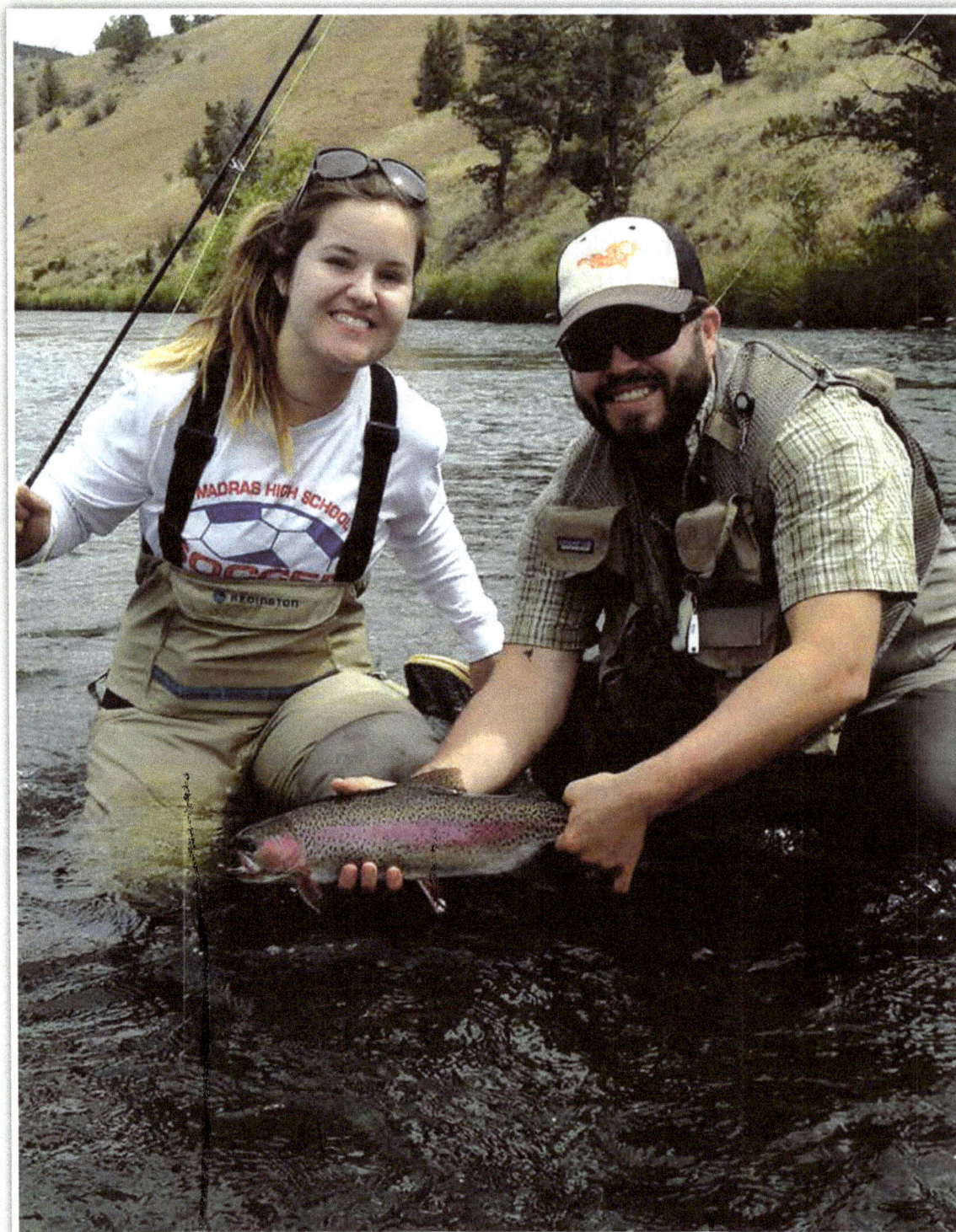

*The now grown siblings, Jordan and Abigail, enjoy the thrill
of catching and returning to the river a colorful native rainbow.*

RELISHING CHILDREN AND RELEASING FISH

"TOO MANY TIMES WE STAND aside and let the waters slip away, till what we put off till tomorrow has now become today."

As a parent and a fisherman, one can think of no greater pleasure than to share the fishing experience with a son or daughter. Certainly, there is something to be said for the male- or female-bonding fishing experience, or solitary retreats to one's fishing haunts, but in the great scheme of things, there is something magical and enduring about enjoying a day on the water with one's offspring.

To be sure, there are certain children or children at certain stages that makes the experience somewhat of a drill, but if handled properly even the most difficult outings can be considered a growth experience and have some redeeming value for both parties (easy to say from the writing table). Much has been written on how to introduce children into the fishing experience. But whether it is a case of "easier said than done" or the fact that much has been unread regarding kids and fishing, it can be a challenge, and you must be able to readjust your goals and tempo when you head out, side by side, to the shore of a lake or stream.

Having five children, I speak not with authority, but with some experience. Each child has been different and while some have discovered the pleasures of fishing, well, the others were less taken with the experience. I am not sure whether it has been an innate quality or had to do with the fact that some were introduced to the excitement of diving bobbers on warm summer days and others, at least one, to fishless days on a steelhead stream in the dead of winter. There is a lesson in there somewhere.

And, of course, there is that issue of finding the time to spend time together. Some kids, in general, are "squeaky wheels" and their persistence leads to activities together. Some, by nature, are reserved and don't share their desires. In our busy lives, without scheduling specific events, times together just don't happen. "When you comin' home, Dad?" "I don't know when, but we'll get together then, son, you know we'll have a good time then." Harry Chapin in his song "Cat's in the Cradle" shares a great insight into the importance of taking the time to spend time together at all stages in life, particularly in the early, formative years.

We have a lot of opportunities to teach our children about life while sharing outdoor experiences. Leaving things in their natural state or putting things back so that others may enjoy them later – be it fish, trees, or the unpicked flower – is certainly a lesson to be passed on.

Catch and release is one of those so-called lessons. It is, however, a hard concept for a little guy to understand when bringing food home for the family is almost a rite of passage. And even though the concept leaves something to be desired, it still represents preservation for the future. So when my youngest boy, Jordan, turned to me while we were fly fishing and asked me why we had to release our fish, I answered him by writing him a poem.

Iowa native, Bud Beamer, saying "thanks" and allowing this rainbow to slip from his hands. Jim Schollmeyer.

Why We Let Fish Go

As I knelt down by the water's edge
to set a rainbow free,
my little boy slid up alongside
and said most sincerely,

"Dad, why work so hard to catch a trout
only to unhook and release?
Why don't we ever take some home
and have a fish-fry feast?"

"Well, I felt the same when I was your age
back there in Iowa," I said.
"We caught quite a few and fried them up,
but they were just perch and bullhead."

"But trout, young fella," I said to my boy
as I placed my hand on his head,
"have a magical quality all of their own
that goes away when they're dead."

"A trout is a beautiful, graceful fish
that can take your breath away.
The way that it leaps to take a fly
then falls back in a splendid spray.*

---

* A paraphrase from an article by Steve Raymond

Fight over, touched coup', back to business. Jim Schollmeyer.

"The natural world that it lives in
makes us want to learn more and more.
The bugs it eats, the hours it keeps,
And the reams of fishing lore.

"Many people work together
to keep our rivers cold and clear,
so that the trout will have a perfect home
and there their offspring rear.

"When you grow up and children have
and they want to fish for rainbow,
and they stand by you and wait for trout,
you'll be glad that we let them go.

"The trout, therefore, are friends of ours;
they add a lot to our lives.
So let's think more of letting them go
and less of tasty fish-fries."

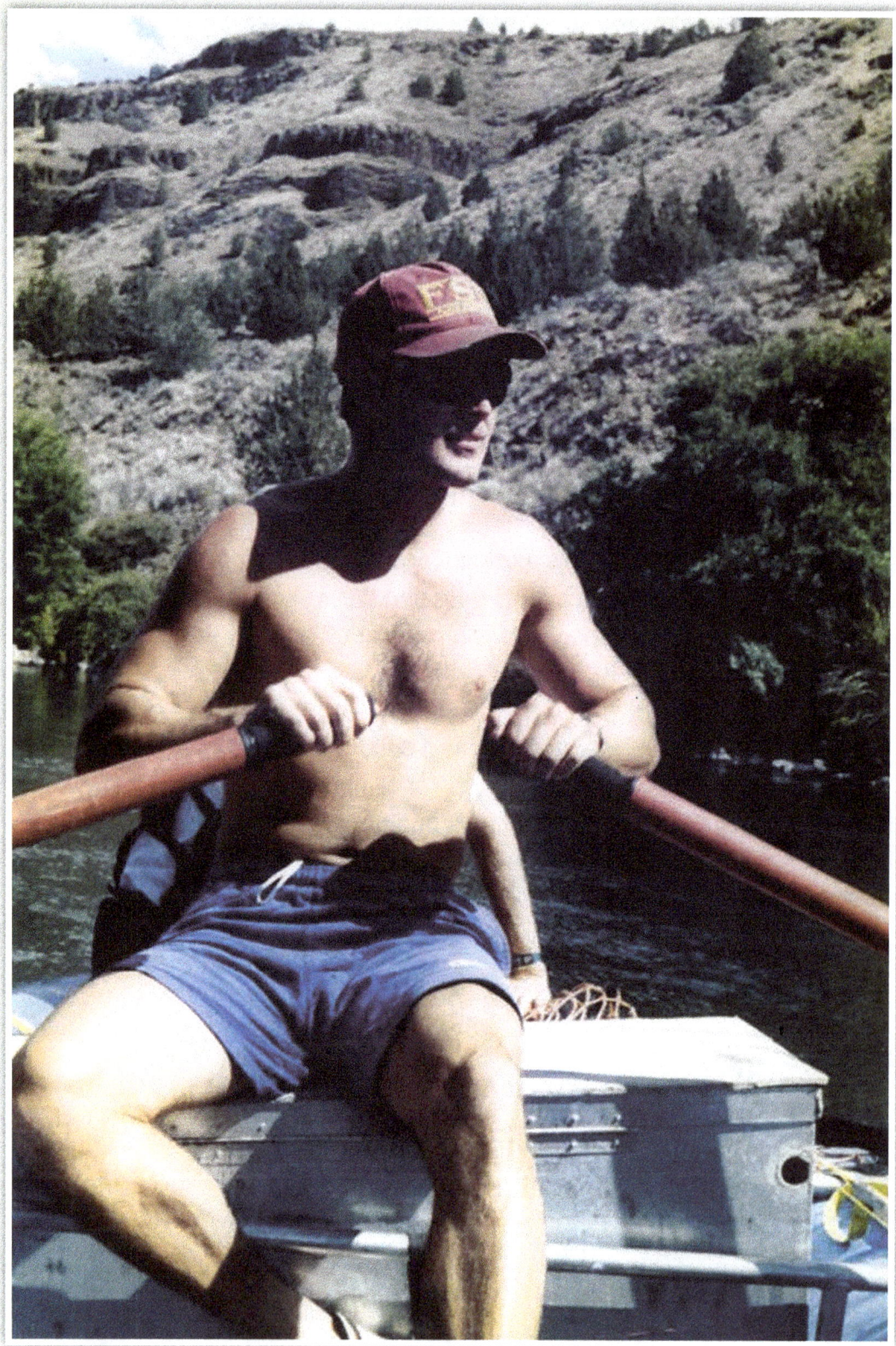

Todd, enjoying the river that he loved.

PART II: RUNNING RIVERS

SOME OF MY FONDEST MEMORIES and greatest getaways, away from electronic devices, highways, and airports, have occurred on the rivers of the Northwest.

In a DC 10 some thirty thousand feet up, these snake-like natural structures appear as innate gunmetal threads, winding between the hills and snow-capped mountains.

All the rivers, regardless of size, flow with similar patterns; the stretches of white water, the multitude of turns and switchbacks, sometimes almost reversing directions, the eddies, the flats; the creeks a microcosm of the larger flows.

Looking down at the rivers, I have flashbacks of rafts and drift boats laden with camping and fishing gear. Rockstrewn rapids, vertical hikes, rod-bending fish, and the gatherings at the end of the day all come to mind. The Deschutes, the John Day, the Snake, the Middle Fork of the Salmon, the Rogue – each has left its indelible mark on us.

Remembering the incredible night sky, the sounds of the river, the occasional wail of a distant train, helps intensify the emotion of the recall. The fragrance of the vegetation, the smell of Russian olive trees, sagebrush, wild roses, the surrounding pines; each river with its own unique memorable ambient bouquet.

Many have enjoyed the thrills and spills and times together. Many will also recall when things didn't go as planned. A few wisps of black clouds coming over the hills proved to be harbingers of some nasty weather. A bright, warm summer day turned into chaos as a howling wind, accompanied with a torrential rain and sleet, punctuated with lightning so close that our hair lifted off of our heads, sent us running for cover with a few more gray hairs.

A flipped raft with loss of gear was also stressful, but having survived that frightful episode, and thanks to a good deal of luck, anxiety and shock were displaced by a certain amount of machismo as the heroic story was shared with others.

Letting your whiskers grow, missing a few baths, using some infrequently used muscles, singing a few songs in front of the campfire, sipping hot, granular "cowboy coffee," and learning new river-running skills are all part of the escape.

It's important that our kids and future generations understand the value of the natural world. Sharing a river trip with family and friends, with or without a dunk in the river, helps all involved create substantive, lasting memories as well as a greater understanding of the importance of preserving this natural resource.

May the decisions of mankind and Laws of Nature continue to provide the high elevations with the snowpack and conditions to keep the rivers full and flowing.

A whole lot of screaming going on. Bruce Bischof, et. al.

Therapeutic Rapids

"So don't sit upon the shoreline and say you're satisfied, choose to chance the rapids and dare to dance the tide."

Running whitewater in a kayak, drift boat, or rubber raft
can be a blend of beauty and pure fright.
But the fear is wholesome, unadulterated, and cleansing,
as the tensions of everyday life are displaced.

The roar of the rapids, as deafening as an oncoming freight train,
the standing waves, suck holes, and hydraulic forces,
pit one against the tempestuous forces of nature,
bringing sweat to the palms and a knot in the gut.

The rodeo of bucking, lurching, and holding on,
submersion and cold-water drenching,
teetering and tipping, diving, falling, and thrashing,
hanging on and gasping for air.

Shouts of instruction, fear, and desperation
turn to healthy sounds of exhilaration.
Another daunting rapids has met its match.
We are alive and glad of it!

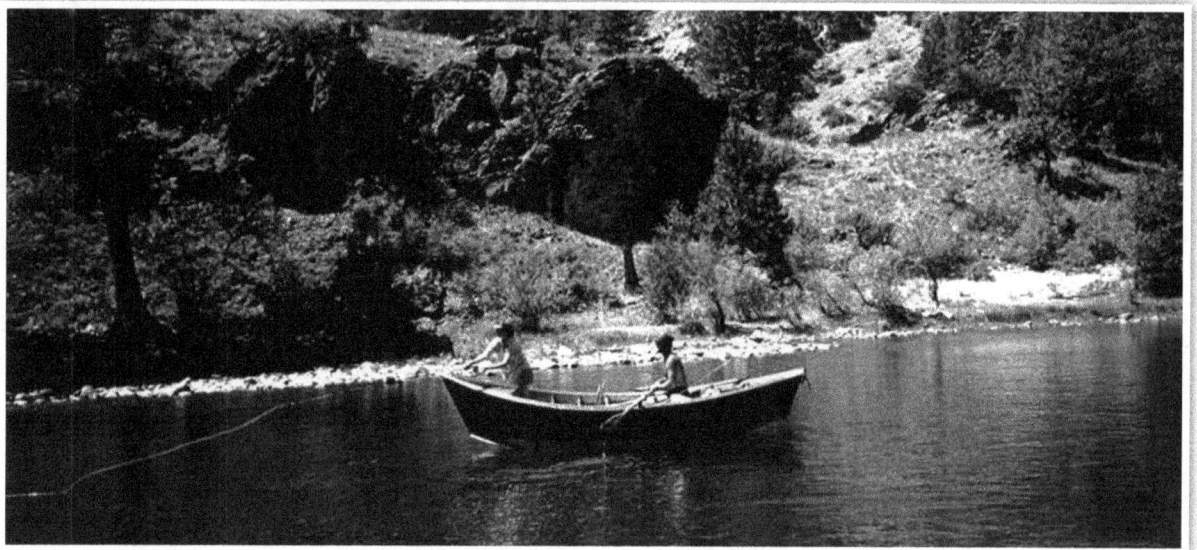

*Working the river for a cutthroat, a couple takes advantage
of some rare quiet waters. Bruce Bischof, et. al.*

Hooked on the Middle Fork

"Like a bird upon the wind, these waters are my sky."

To cast a fly on a river you love
can right the world you live in.
To escape to waters that stir your soul
can cleanse the self within.

Drifting a river with rod in hand,
employing one's fly-casting skills;
holding on through waters white,
a marvelous blend of thrills.

Such can be found in a glorious place
at the nadir of a deep canyon,
where unspoiled nature demands attention,
on the Middle Fork of the Salmon.

The fish are there with blood red gills,
to be caught and released with a "thanks,"
for the thrill of seeing them leap and run,
performing along bouldered banks.

A menu tied on their behalf
can be cast from a boat or in waders.
Royalty reigns with a Coachman or Wulf
or bodacious stimulators.

Few things in life spawn pleasant dreams
as does this drift of pleasure.
Beauty without becomes beauty within,
transformed by this natural treasure.

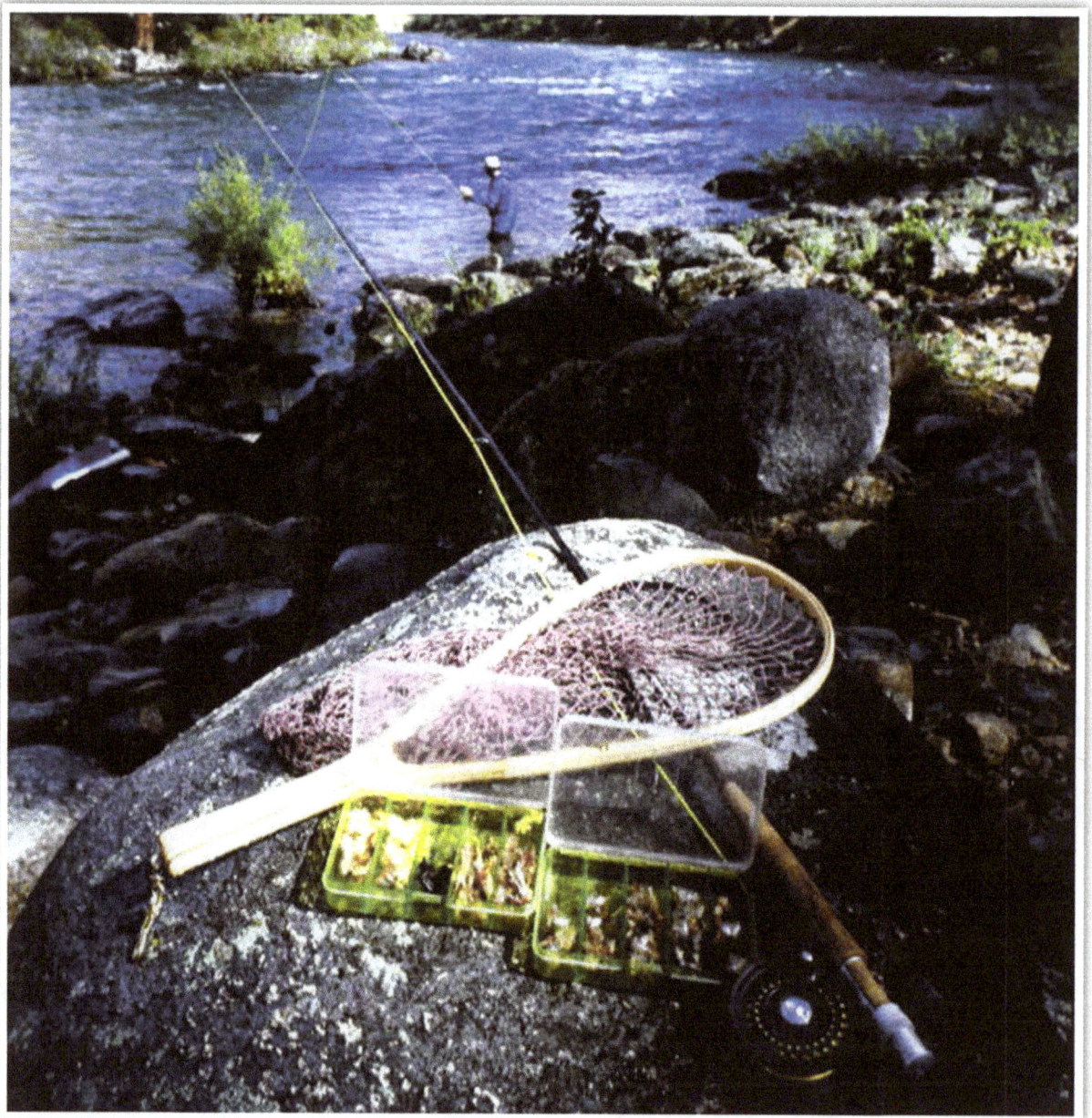

A fisherman's dream: beauty, solitude, and a river with abundant Cutthroat Trout. Bischof, et. al.

A Morning hike takes two brothers, Jordan and Todd, to the top plateau of the Middle Fork Canyon. Todd Beamer camera.

This poem was written for the exquisite picture book entitled *The Middle Fork of The Salmon River* authored by Bruce Bischof.

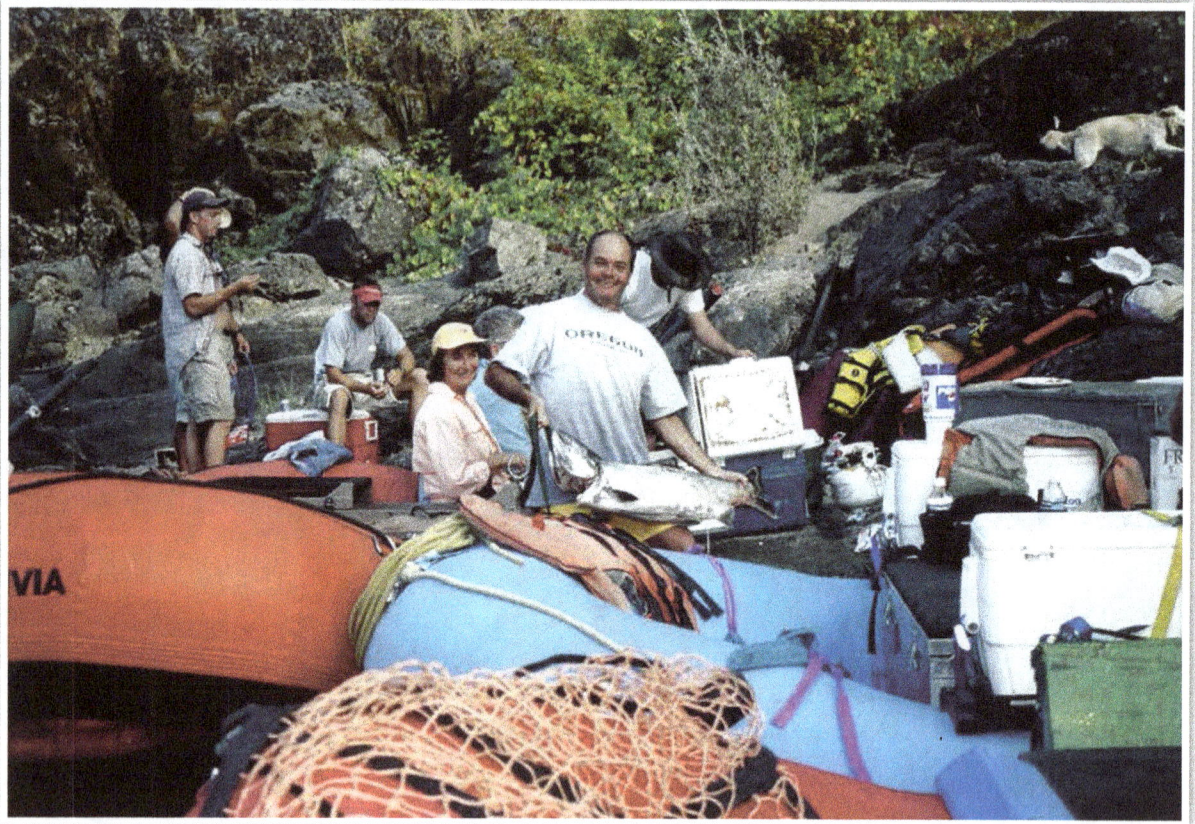

A Rogue River pullout is even more fun with a fresh Salmon on board. Author.

Cuckoo on the River

I've been knocked "cuckoo" a few times.
Cuckoo being the operative word here.
Hitting the diving board with my head and
falling off a haystack, to name a few.

These episodes were pretty straightforward,
the natural law of gravity taking effect.
But there has been a time or two when
pure stupidity went into play

Take for instance the time on the Rogue River;
certainly, the most beautiful of river trips.
My wife was running the framed rubber raft
in a seemingly quiet stretch of the river.

Being a fly fisherman, I took the opportunity
to stand behind her and cast from the raft.
To avoid chafing, I took my life jacket off
and began casting toward the river's seams.

Kids love the river trips and sometimes things get a little "cuckoo."
The Kemper kids and Todd having a morning rinse. Author.

The river's famed steelhead summer run was in progress
and I figured that I'd test Zane Grey's favorite waters.
He had fished from shore and, being smart,
would have used caution in all his efforts.

Casting from a rubber raft without a life jacket
defied good sense and my wife's warnings.
An isolated standing wave broke the calm surface.
"Just point towards it and row away."

Like a siren calling, it sucked us into its trough.
I reeled forward as she recoiled backward.
Our heads collided, my cheekbone against her occiput.
The lights went out, the birdies sang.

I landed on the oar and flipped it from its moorage.
My wife and oar-lock spared me from the river,
my axilla wrapped around the forged U of steel.
I would live to see another day.

I awoke to screams and a frightened family.
My lost fly rod was my first concern.
A 7-weight Sage with a Ross Reel is no small loss,
and some great steelhead water lay ahead.

An extra oar took my place on the oar-lock
and we headed toward our third day's camp.
I was pretty quiet the rest of the trip.
My wife states that I was actually more fun.

I missed the fishing, but it didn't seem important.
Thanks to Aleve, I relaxed and enjoyed the river.
The surroundings, the company was all I could ask for.
Normal birdsongs were also appreciated.

Plenty of "cowboy coffee" coming up. Jim Rozewski.

A Rogue River camp with the family makes up for some earlier pratfalls. Bud and Beth Ann with Jennie, Annie, and Jordan, who is sporting his self-cut bangs.

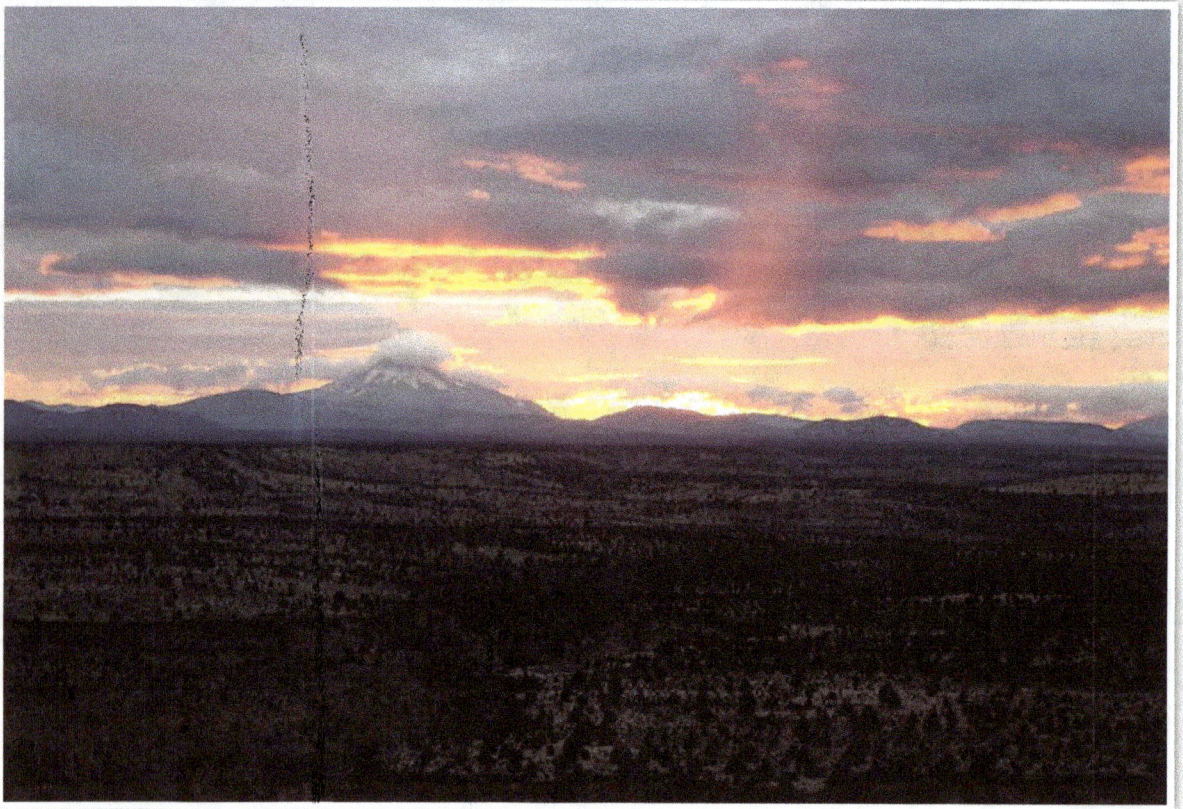

The day celebrates it's ending with an array of fiery colors. Author.

PART III: PASSIONS

OUR HOME AND RANCH ARE located on a cliff that overlooks the last impoundment of the Deschutes River as it begins its final hundred-mile stretch to the Columbia River. It is a spiritual setting, as the Cascade Mountains connect the heavens to the earth. A vast array of sunsets confirms this celestial connection.

The ranch extends for one mile along the rim of the canyon, and much of our ranch life is significantly influenced by the setting and our connection with the river. Managing our hay fields and cattle on the rim, watching flights of water fowl as they pass overhead, observing the birds of prey riding the thermals, and taking regular hikes on the switchback canyon road, with the Deschutes River in full view, are activities that help offset the more arduous tasks. The water that brings our hayfields to life comes from the Deschutes via an elaborate canal system that begins at its headwaters some hundred miles away.

As a family physician and surgeon for forty years, I have tried to keep a balance in my life by blending various activities and challenges with the practice of medicine. We bought the ranch after losing our son, needing some space and connection to the natural world. Being outside doing physical labor, watching the sun rise and set, watching things grow, working with the horses, cattle, and calves has helped the healing process.

I recall the satisfaction I experienced one cold winter night, with the moonlight reflecting off the glaciers on Mt. Jefferson, watching the calves with their tails in the air, skittering around the barnyard like a herd of cats. Even getting up at 0200 to change water brings rewards. Walking through the hayfields with our dogs at my side, looking up at the stars on a moonless night, a surreal peace is experienced.

In his song "The River" Garth sings "and there's bound to be rough waters and I know I'll take some falls, but with the Good Lord as my captain, I can make it through them all." This verse certainly has religious overtones and one's beliefs are each individual's decision. For me personally, it has been a great comfort to not go through life alone and to have someone to help right the ship.

So we find a way to sail our vessel through life, "learning from what's behind us, never knowing what's in store." The natural world and staying emotionally connected in our human relationships can offer buffers that sustain us and keep us moving forward.

I have included some poems that have to do with the human condition and the environment and creatures around us. Some are just a sharing and others have a message that I feel may have some relevance to fishermen and nonfishermen alike.

Not exactly a pot of gold, but certainly a way of life. Author.

Born on a Frosty Morn

It's poor animal husbandry when you breed
your cattle so that they calve in February.
Covered with fluid and dropped on the frost-covered ground
is a thoughtless way to start a life.

The hoarfrost covers the pungent sagebrush,
the juniper branches tipped with frost.
The snow-capped mountains oversee the process
with a cold indifference to the baby's plight.

The first-time mother seems confused
as to what has exited her exhausted body.
She longs for water and green alfalfa flakes
awaiting her in the adjacent field.

She looks behind at the wet lump of coal
that lies shivering in the cold morning air.
If she leaves, the calf is doomed; the cold
and coyotes will seal his fate.

But instinctively she turns around
and investigates this newborn creature.
She sniffs and smells; the matchless scent
locks forever in her brain.

Country Road with its many switchbacks descends to the Deschutes with Mt. Jefferson in full view. Author.

She licks the wet black coat with her
rough tongue made of muscle.
The coat dries and the stimulated calf
begins to respond and warm.

The jittery baby tries to stand
but falls head first into the ground.
Three times he fails to gain his feet,
his wobbly legs collapsing beneath him.

He rights himself and migrates back
to his mother's underbelly.
Instinct, like a magnet, the drawing force
that helps ensure survival.

The clueless heifer is confused
and repeatedly kicks him away.
The desperate calf searching, seeking
as the clock is ticking.

The dense, rich fluid that she carries
is essential for his health.
The next few hours are critical
if his body is to absorb the nutrient.

Never argue with a protective mother cow. Author.

His persistence finally pays off,
the mother accepting her dutiful role.
He latches on, he nurses eagerly.
The colostrum will fortify and protect.

They constitute a pair, this now proud mother
and handsome calf.
She will protect him at all costs,
and select him out among the many.

The calf will eventually receive his shots,
castration, and the woeful weaning.
He has survived his ill-timed birth
and will romp with look-alikes in the herd.

From the porch, we view the geese heading south with the Three Sisters and Brokentop in background. Author.

Late Summer Geese

I know that summer is coming to an end.
The Canada geese are flying.
Coming and going from the lake below, their
distinguishing sound fills the air.

Whether at home or on the river
their presence in sound or sight is felt.
One dares not look up when fishing.
"Bombs away" I believe is the term.

They barely clear our rock home perched
high on the basalt rim.
Our attention turns toward the pink morning
sky as they pass overhead.

They are already in formation,
only moments after taking off,
left wing behind right wing on one side.
right behind left on the other.

They are headed for the Oregon wheat fields,
grain recently winnowed from the land.
They are in luck, for golden kernels of grain
have inadvertently been left for them.

They find the center of the field
away from natural and unnatural enemies.
A sentry or two keeps watch.
All heads up if the alarm sounds.

Dining done, they lift off and once again
clear the rim of fluted rock.
Like jet planes wafting back and forth,
they descend to the lake below.

The hours that they keep
seem irregular by our standards.
Migrating geese often fly at night,
perhaps to escape the daytime winds.

Loading hay one night, I hear the
cacophony of incessant honking.
Looking up, I see the perfect V
pass before the full moon.

I sit and watch and wonder what goes through
the mind of a goose in flight.
Does he look down and wonder why I am
loading hay at this time of night.

Or is he following certain instincts that direct
him to some Southern clime
where open waters and less frigid breezes await.
A safer haven which promises a return.

Spring time brings warmer weather and relief from freezing temperatures. Author.

Drain, baby, drain. Author.

Hoses in the Trees

When winter strikes and temperatures
plummet to subzero marks,
those caught unprepared pay the price,
when lines of water become tubes of ice.

Ranch animals are left restless and confused
as they stare at troughs of solid water.
"Bring out the hoses" is our battle cry,
as our breath freezes in the air.

We learn that this is more than a one-time fix
when hoses are left undrained.
"Thaw them in the bathtub!" becomes our
next early morning cry.

Friends now ask "Why are hoses hanging
high up in your trees?"
For hoses in trees are a bizarre addition
to a winter ranch scene.

Christmas lights would be much more
attractive and seasonal.
But gravity-drained hoses have their own beauty,
with peace of mind thrown in.

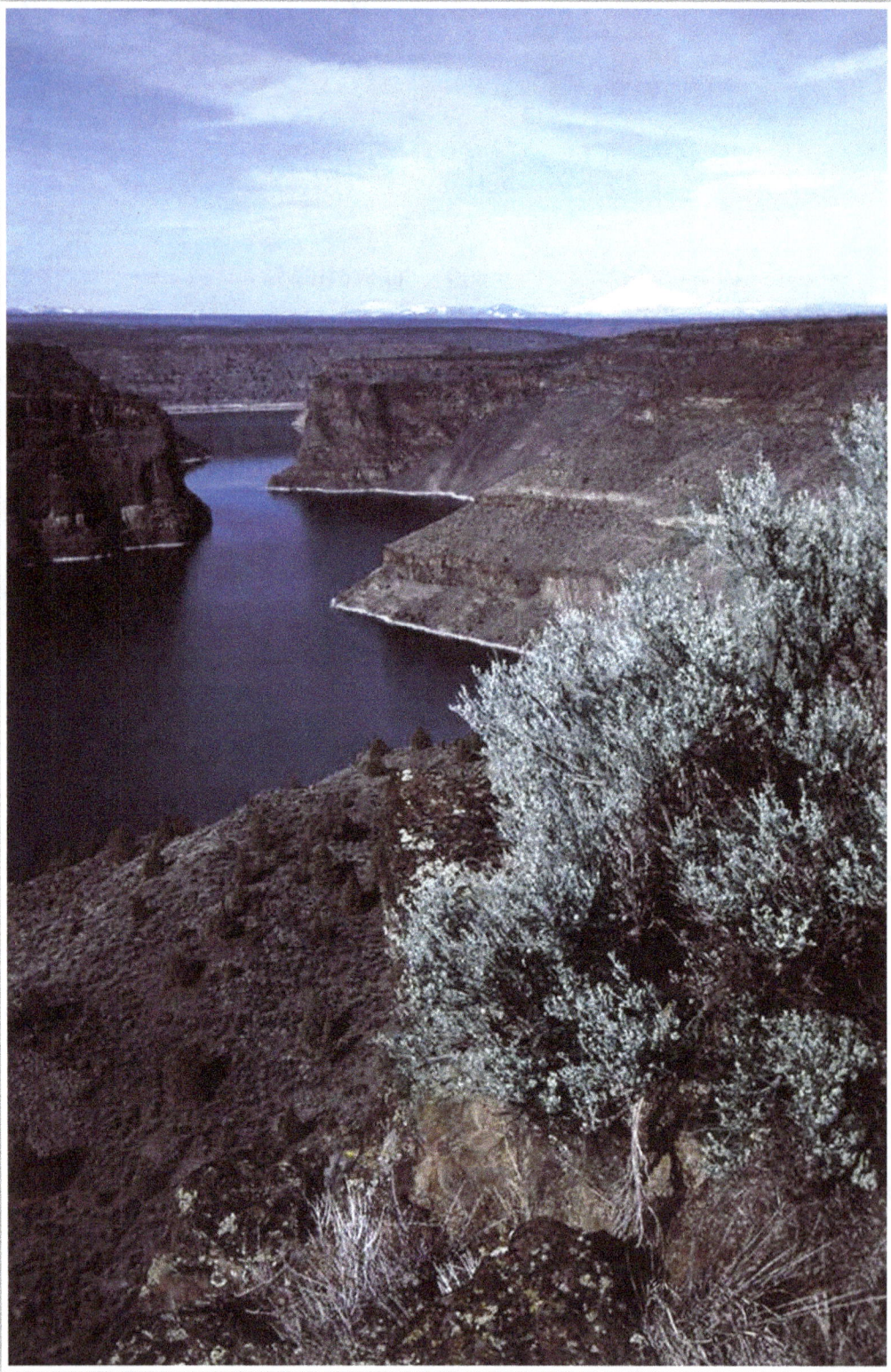

Billy Chinook Mt. Hood. David V. Evans

Reunions

Another reunion is on the agenda.
Whether to go is always the question.
I don't think that I ever regretted attending,
for friends and memories are more than precious.

Maybe the brain in younger years wires itself
to relationships and music of the time.
Faces and songs stir a sentiment
that makes you feel alive and more.

Earlier gatherings are fun and informative
as we compare and impress.
As years go by we value each other
and miss those who aren't there.

The hair, the teeth, the weight, the skin,
a lot of changes can take place.
It doesn't matter; your classmates are there,
and appreciated more than ever.

It's like a production of Our Town
with makeup, crow's feet, wrinkled hands.
But the voice, the laugh, they haven't changed.
It's yester-year, not years later.

The pictures of our deceased classmates
are posted so that they're remembered.
Some lived hard and took so many risks;
others did everything right and still lost the battle.

What transpired since those fun-filled days,
when not a care existed?
Why didn't someone warn us then
that life was hard and we'd be tested?

That's why coming back can mean so much
for those who traveled near and far,
who will experience the profound effect
that comes from rekindling long-lost feelings.

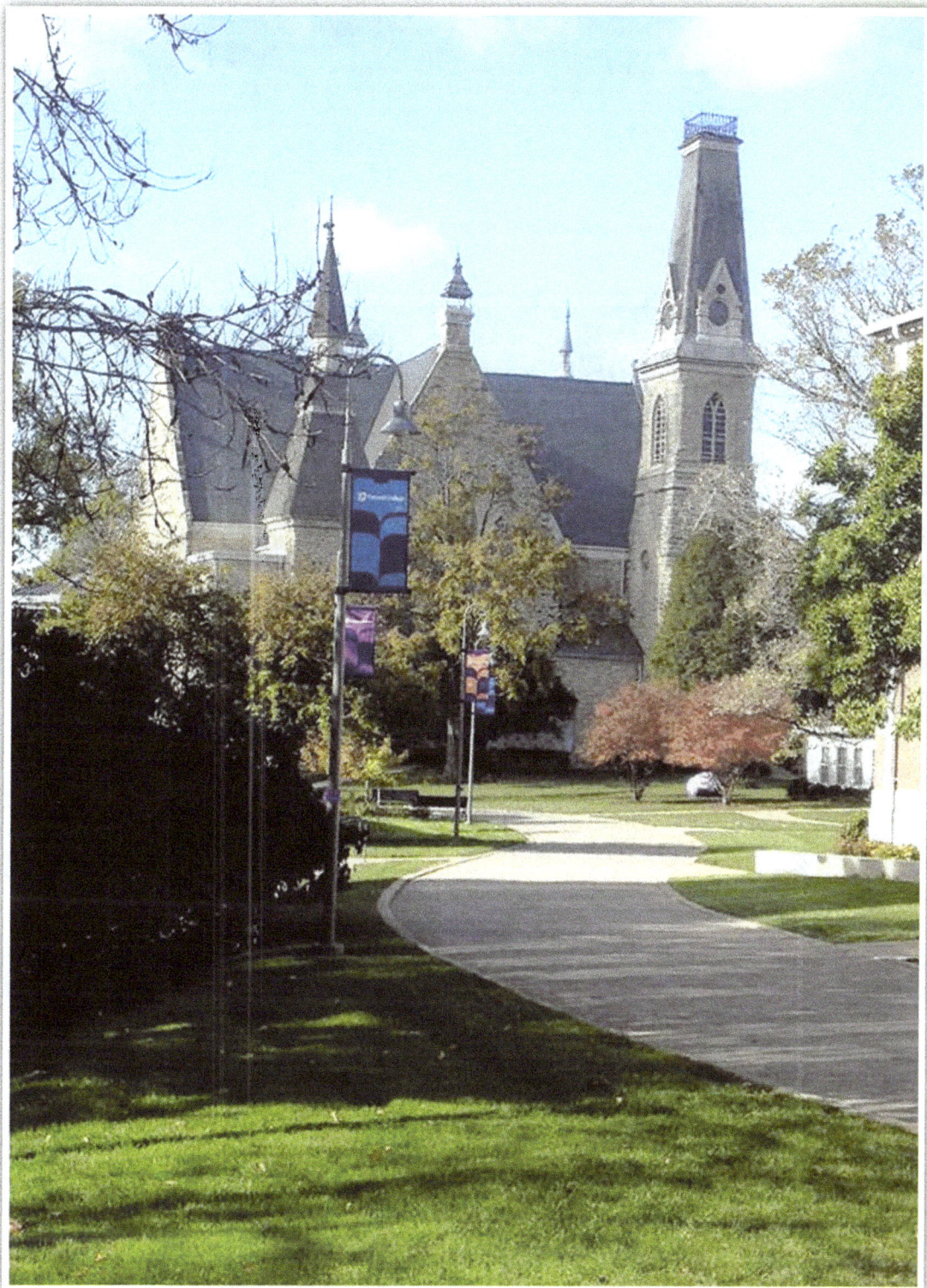

King Chapel, which dominates the landscape at Cornell College,
stirs memories for alumni who return for reunions.

The Metolius River, created from the great lava water storage system of the Cascades, offers beauty and challenging fishing as it flows to join the Deschutes. David V. Evans.

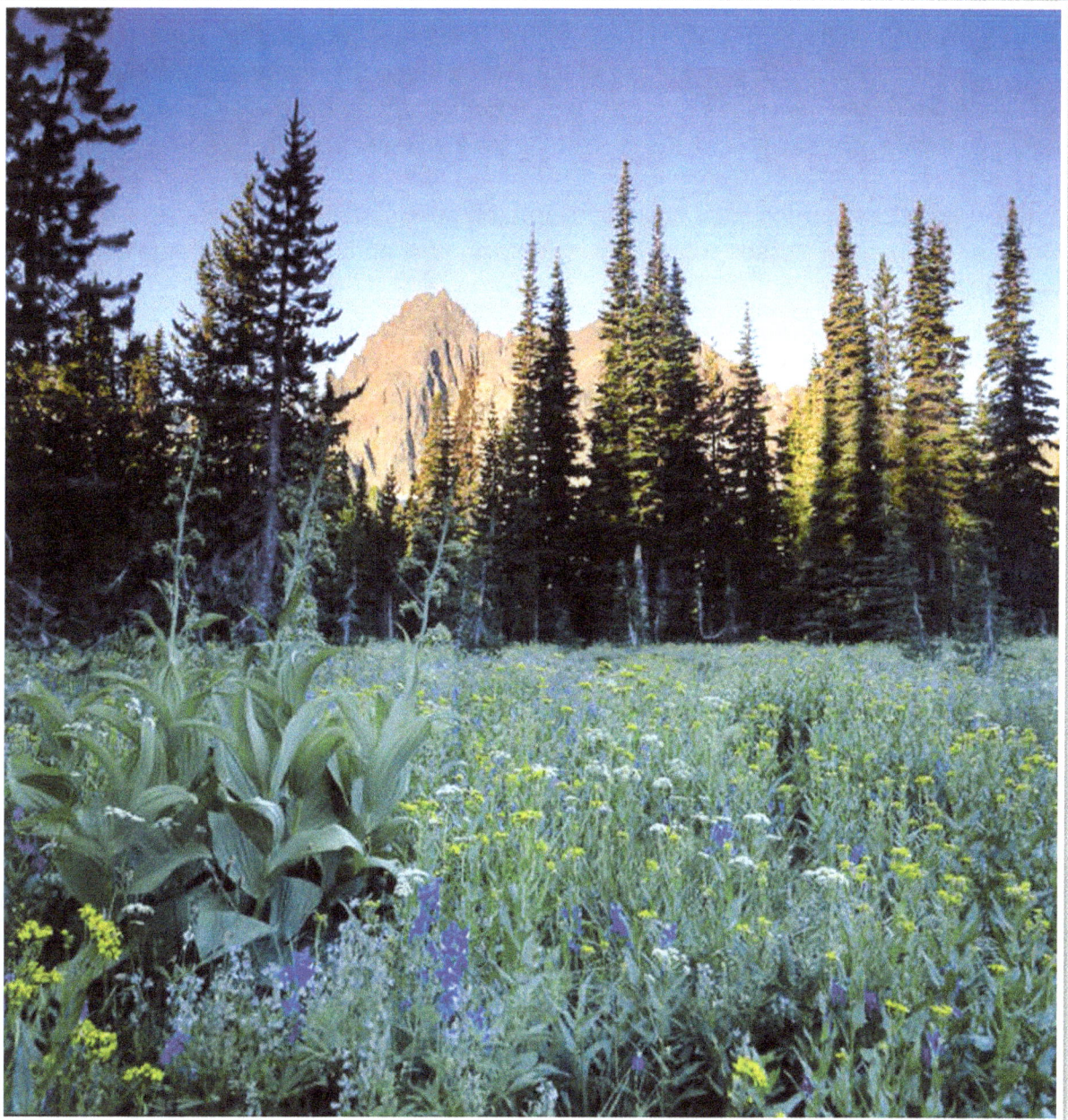

Canyon Creek Meadow is one of a number of beautiful settings that makes a hike in the Cascades a most worthwhile afternoon adventure. David V. Evans.

WHY WE ARE WHO WE ARE

THE NATURAL WORLD PRESENTS MANY metaphors that relate to the human condition. We have a crooked, gnarly tree in front of our fishing lodge that every year comes closer to tipping into the river. Its unique distorted shape helps bring to mind the Gaelic proverb "It's not easy to straighten in the oak the crook that grew in the sapling."

I have had a passion for early childhood development since my college days at Cornell College, when my professor spoke convincingly on how early beginnings determined who we would become.

A considerable amount of research has been done since then that actually shows the absence of critical pathways in the brains of infants subjected to stress or indifference. The pathways that control the centers for empathy and self-regulation are most vulnerable to the stress chemicals cortisol and norepinephrine, and are destroyed and pruned from the brain.

Consequently, there is a reason why some become altruistic, caring human beings while others commit heinous acts and endorse man's inhumanity to man. Whether individuals will become contributing members of society or will wear down our social and legal systems is determined by the amount of nurturing and caring that they receive in those formative "sapling" years.

The fact that there are multifold increases in chronic disease states, addiction, mental illness, and learning disabilities in those individuals who experienced dysfunctional, stressful starts to their lives makes it imperative that prevention and education measures be addressed.

Anyone that is involved with raising and caring for children needs to be aware of the relationship between a caring environment and the development of the brain.

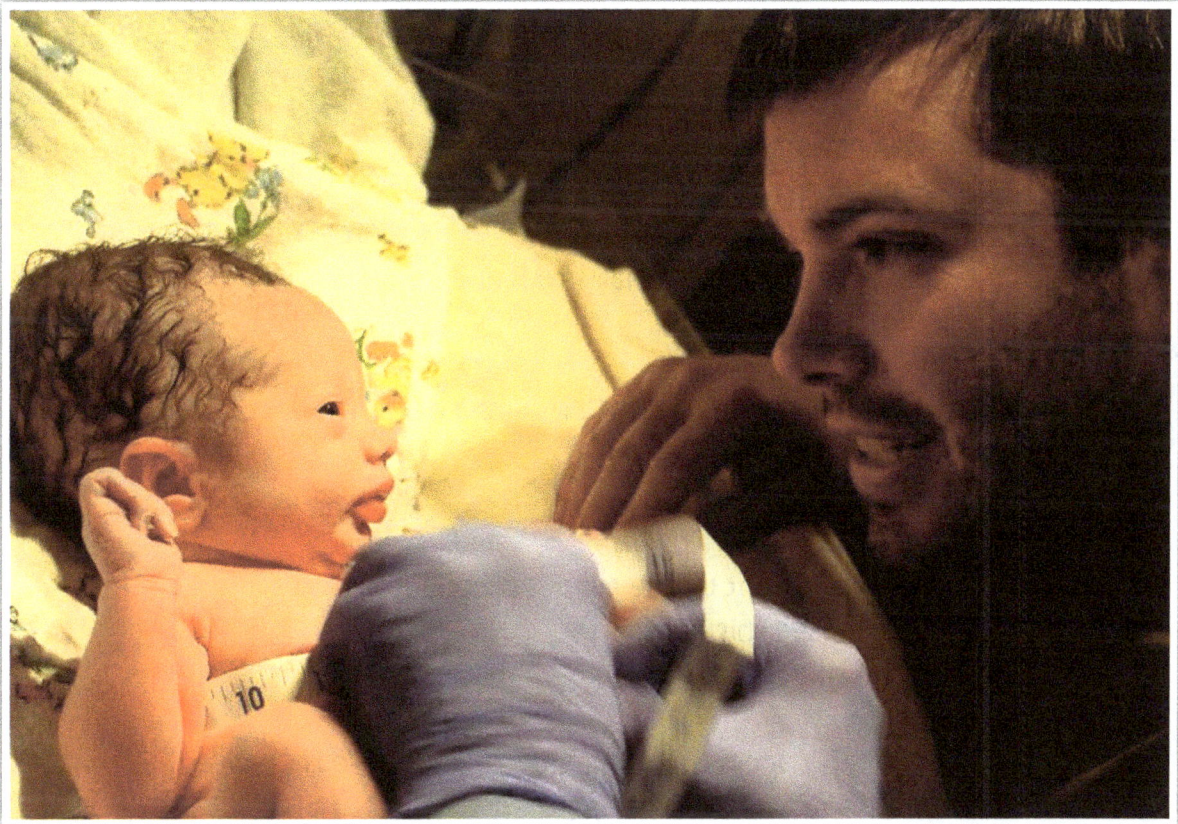

Jordan and Baby Grace. It is never too early to start eye connection and attachment. Author.

Hungry Eyes

Their hungry eyes look and search
for a face that looks at them,
looking back.

Eyes connect and a soul is filled with a surge
of warmth and excitement unmatched by food
or other comforts.

If only each and every baby would find this source
of caring eyes and a face that smiles and
a voice that sings.

Would not her face be full of smiles and her
precious mind thrive and grow
to do good things?

The eyes of a parent whose mind is preoccupied
may not truly see this baby or be
received in such a way.

And losing this opportunity, a baby's precious life is changed
and who she was to be is but a ghost*
that follows her now lesser life.

There is that time, so critical and urgent, when hungry eyes
and growing minds will reflect and thrive, and then
this time will cease.

Let us be aware and let us care to act, support,
and advocate for those who have no voice and
whose life in some way will affect us all.

---

*a reference to Ghosts *From The Nursery,* Karr-Morse & Wiley: Atlantic Monthly

Astor flowers beautify the surrounding area of Todd Lake that lies northwest of Mt. Bachelor. David V. Evans.

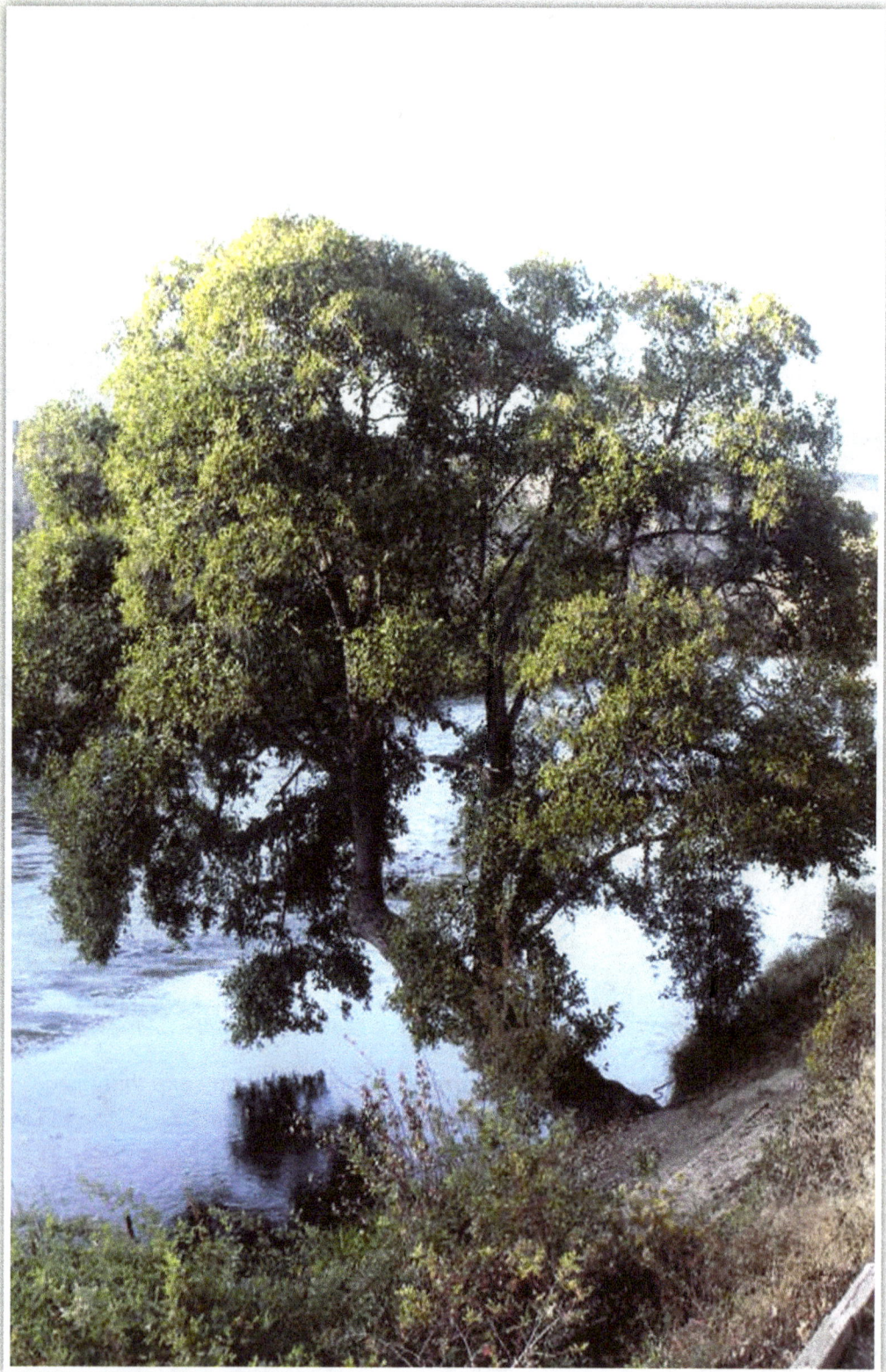

A gnarly streamside tree. The crook started in the sapling.

Within the Prison Walls

Inmates need to be held accountable
for the bad things they have done.
Society needs be protected
from those that pose a threat.

There are, however, questions
that still remain unanswered.
Were individuals born innately bad
or did they develop that way?

Some were affected by events
while still within the womb.
Others may have, by chance, been born
into chaos or indifference.

Is it not unfair to start life
with one foot in the bucket?
And to be judged by others
who had a much better beginning?

We know now why some live life
without empathy for others.
We also understand why bad habits form
to calm the inner storms.

The brain with millions of pathways
is a reflection of one's environment,
a template that forms in response
to interactions in one's surroundings.

If love and nurturing are there,
a caring human will join the ranks;
an individual who will contribute
and make the world a better place.

Toxic stress will rob the infant
of this hope and of this chance.
Kindness and caring displaced
by human disregard and disrespect.

An inmate may have no remorse
for egregious acts he carried out,
or misuse drugs and alcohol
to calm his frazzled mind.

Intrinsic values, a moral compass,
entities so apparently lacking.
Right from wrong, known by most,
but not a concern in times of decision.

Some parents did the best they could
and still their children went astray.
Other parents did nothing right
and yet their children found their way.

If inmates' parents had been mine
and mine in turn were theirs,
would I now be judged by them
and find myself within the walls?

Knowing the origins of human failure,
we should promote effective measures,
so parents raising children understand
the essential needs of those beginning life.

The stark figure of a burned Juniper tree stands watch over the Crooked River and picturesque Smith Rock formation. The latter was formed when the major tributary of the Deschutes was blocked by lava flows and the river, in time, carved what is today a renowned, world-class rock climbing and hiking area. David V. Evans.

PART IV: DEDICATION

I HAVE DEDICATED THIS LITTLE book of poems and prose to my mother, Elizabeth Evans Beamer, and our son, Todd Evans Beamer, whom we lost in a drowning accident at the age of twenty-eight.

As I mentioned in the introduction, I strongly believe that my passion for fishing came from my mother. I remember the fall afternoon when I was taking her to the Portland Airport for her return flight back to Iowa. We had stopped at our fishing cabin so that I could try a new fly that a friend had hand-tied for me – a variation of the Leadeyed Wooly bugger. I hooked a good-sized steelhead out in front of the cabin. As I struggled to land him, I could hear her talking to our lodge host, Norma Jordan, who was with her on the deck, and saying, "Oh, I hope and pray that he can land him. The poor boy works so hard and this would give him such relief." Only a loving mother says such things. She loved the color purple and the poem "Purple" is dedicated to her memory.

Todd loved the natural world and even as a college student took up the cause to preserve the salmon runs – the "silver thread that binds the Northwest together." Central Oregon, with its multitude of outdoor activities, provided us with many opportunities to spend time together. Running rivers, snowboarding, long-distance running, and, of course, fishing were major pursuits. "A Place in the Stream" was composed to honor these memories.

Mother's death was from natural causes. Todd drowned trying to save our four dogs that were caught in a siphon. While challenging our faith, his death helped us to understand the process of life. Although we are not Jewish, the writings of Rabbi Harold Kushner helped us immensely. He helped us understand God's role in our lives and that God gave us the gift of life as well as the conditions of life. Random acts, the laws of nature, as well as, in Todd's case, the fact that we are morally free to make our own choices, all create a double-edged sword. As we experienced, all the beauty around us can be shattered by the conditions of life. God limits Himself in these realms so that life can continue in an orderly fashion. Our faith is restored by the God-like qualities in mankind that just don't come from anywhere. The outpouring of human caring was immense and helped us move forward.

The lives of both Mother and Todd helped us to understand that we can make a difference in each other's lives and that the ripple effect of positive action goes on and on and gives eternalness to our existence.

Purple—one of nature's most delicate and beautiful colors—and memories. Author.

Purple

The smell of spring is here again.
The lilac fragrance strikes a chord.
A sob emits from some inner source
with thoughts of a mother so adored.

She had sung in spring she would not leave.
From Camelot the words had come.
And yet in spring she did depart;
the music stilled, the singing done.

She had missed my call on Mother's Day.
My card had come with words of praise.
But there is so much I would have said
on that the last of mother's days.

The telephone is less important now.
The voice I long for won't be there.
I loved the calls on Sunday eve,
"Mamma my love," "Buddy my dear."

Music was her greatest gift.
She shared it graciously with others.
She sang, she played, it filled our home
and filled our heart, this gift of mothers.

Balsam Root. The purple flowery background is like a mother's presence—
in the life of the yellow Balsam Root. David V. Evans.

She loved her neighbor as herself.
She let them all know that they mattered.
A thoughtful call, a birthday card,
sympathy, if lives were shattered.

She taught me always to be kind,
to always show appreciation;
To lose some battles to win a war;
higher thoughts, determination.

She forgave my faults and indiscretions.
Purple things my love did show.
I did dedicate my life to her.
She sensed I would. Somehow mothers know.

So violets, lilacs, Purple robes,
gestures, gifts that brought a smile.
Purple – that brings her back to me,
and in my heart she stays awhile.

Reeds on river bank. The patch of reeds remains as does the memory. Author.

A Place in the Stream

"I could have missed the pain, but I'd have had
to miss the dance."*

I stood on the deck and looked down
at the patch of reeds.
The river flowing by, mingled its waters
with the green stems.

It was a place my son had knelt
to release a rainbow trout.
I had headed down when I heard
the "big fish!" shout.

The picture I took of the football-sized fish
and that big, proud smile
sits on my desk in the study.
That moment lingers, bittersweet.

We had hoped to fish many more
streams together;
recalling times together, touchdown passes,
years growing up.

The years had flown by, early challenges
transformed to strength and character.
A schoolboy, a teacher and coach,
a future brimming with promise.

---

*   From "The Dance," written and sung by Garth Brooks

A distance run in Central Oregon
had changed all that.
Five dogs, a mountain backdrop, waterfowl,
a canal, flowing toward the canyon siphon.

High water, the soft gravel, an escape impossible.
A delightful romp became a disaster.
"Life doesn't get any better than this"
became "Save the dogs!"

Dogs were swept swiftly toward the canyon.
Cement weirs sealed their fate.
Their master followed, all creatures unconscious,
breathing water instead of air.

The community had responded with tears and hugs,
sentiments, and accolades.
Family, friends, students, and teammates
came to say goodbye and pay respect.

The university gives a memorial award
to a spirited, dedicated athlete.
Todd's death had rocked their football program.
His memory needed to be preserved.

Four years he had played the game he loved,
two more years served as a coach.
He had left everything on the field
on which I painfully threw his ashes.

"Those things that we do for ourselves
die with us.
Those things that we do for others
go on and on."

Words spoken, hoping that what he embodied
would be everlasting.
The ripple effect on the lives he touched
would affect many.

Years have softened the grief
and the ache in my chest has diminished.
His football, his fishing rod, his pictures,
are all poignant reminders.

The river flows by, the endless passage of water.
Todd's ashes are long gone.
From the deck flow fond memories;
a boy, a man, eternally young.

"Todd's icon, the Bald Eagle flies over our home just checking in."

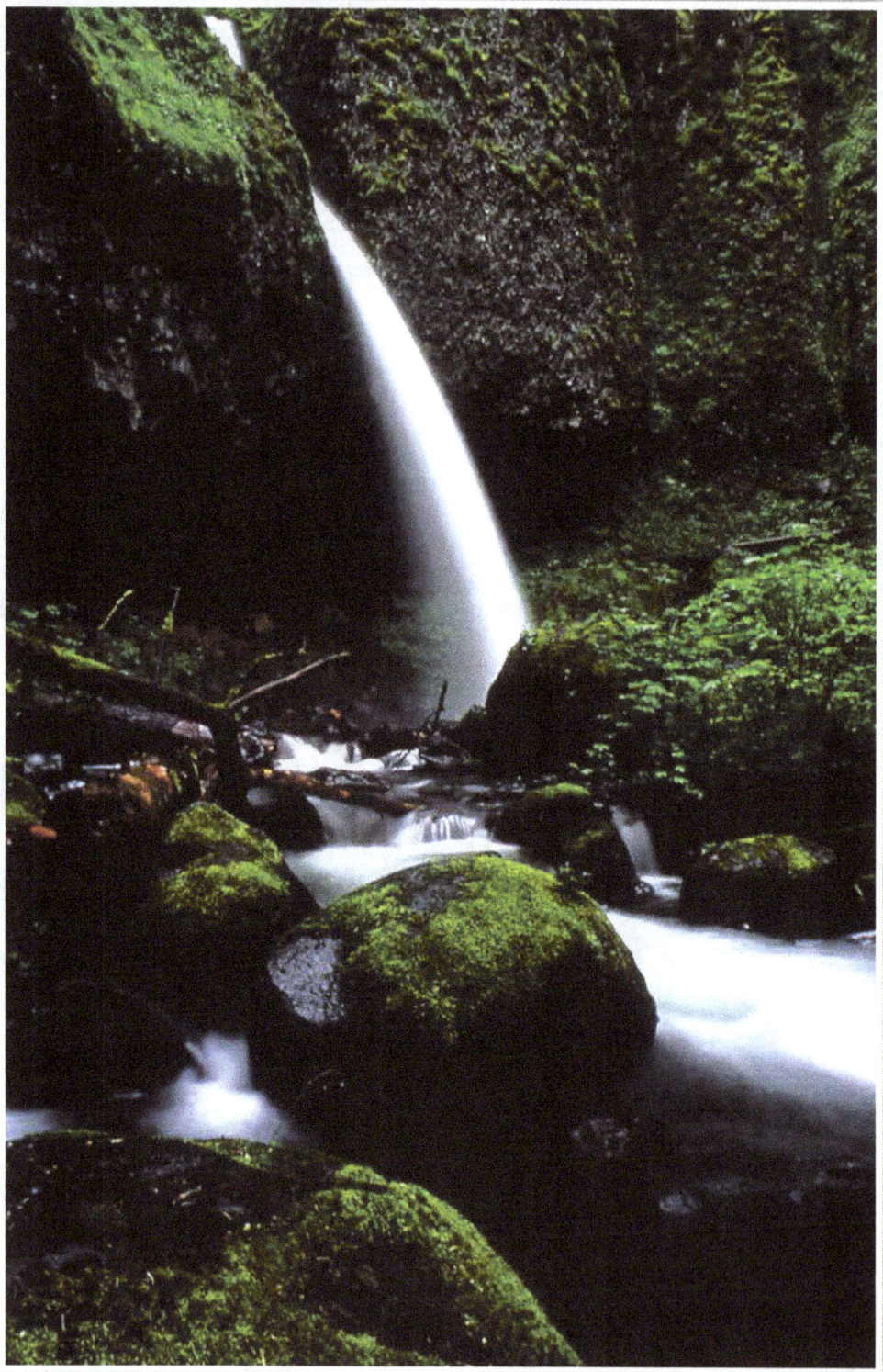

High in the Cascades, the remarkable beauty of the beginnings of a mountain stream can be found. There is splendor all around us. David V. Evans.

EPILOGUE

I APOLOGIZE FOR ENDING THE book on a somewhat gloomy note. The end of life can be a gloomy, oftentimes tragic experience. This book is an expression of what we do with our lives before the finish line.

How do we find fulfillment? How do we make a difference? How do we make the most of what we have? How do we create buffers that offset the disappointments and the nadirs of our rollercoaster life experience?

How do we understand the importance of creating memories? I have lost two fishing buddies, one to cancer, the other to a rare neurologic disease. Our outings together, laughing and sharing, provide a vivid tapestry to my life. My son and I squeezed every bit of juice out of life that we could. I have no regrets.

We all would like to live a meaningful life. "Meaning is something you build into your life. You build it out of your own past, out of your affections and loyalties, out of the experience of humankind as it is passed on to you. Meaning is an uplifting state of consciousness, when you're serving things beyond yourself."*

Each of us finds our own way. You can only control what you put into life. Waiting for someone to help you or expecting that someone else will create your happiness or that only good things will happen to you if you play your cards right can lead to disappointments, disillusionments, and, when things really go wrong, even "knock you off your horse," as they say.

Some of us get a good start in life. Some start life, unfortunately, with one foot in the bucket. The breadth of our experience is also somewhat dependent on our personal resources.

Using good judgment is a critical component when deciding to engage in an outdoor endeavor as it is with all aspects of life. The British mountaineer Edward Whympers stated: "climb if you will, but remember that courage and strength are naught without prudence and that momentary negligence may destroy the happiness of a lifetime. Do nothing in haste, look well to each step, and from the beginning think what may be the end." Some acts are reflexive, but most dreadful events or decisions we make could be avoided if we took these words to heart.

The natural world is available to all of us. Let us enjoy it, be safe, experience the healing qualities it offers, and, above all, preserve it – a moral imperative.

"Yes I will sail my vessel till the river runs dry."

---

*   John Gardner, in a speech to the Stanford Alumni Association

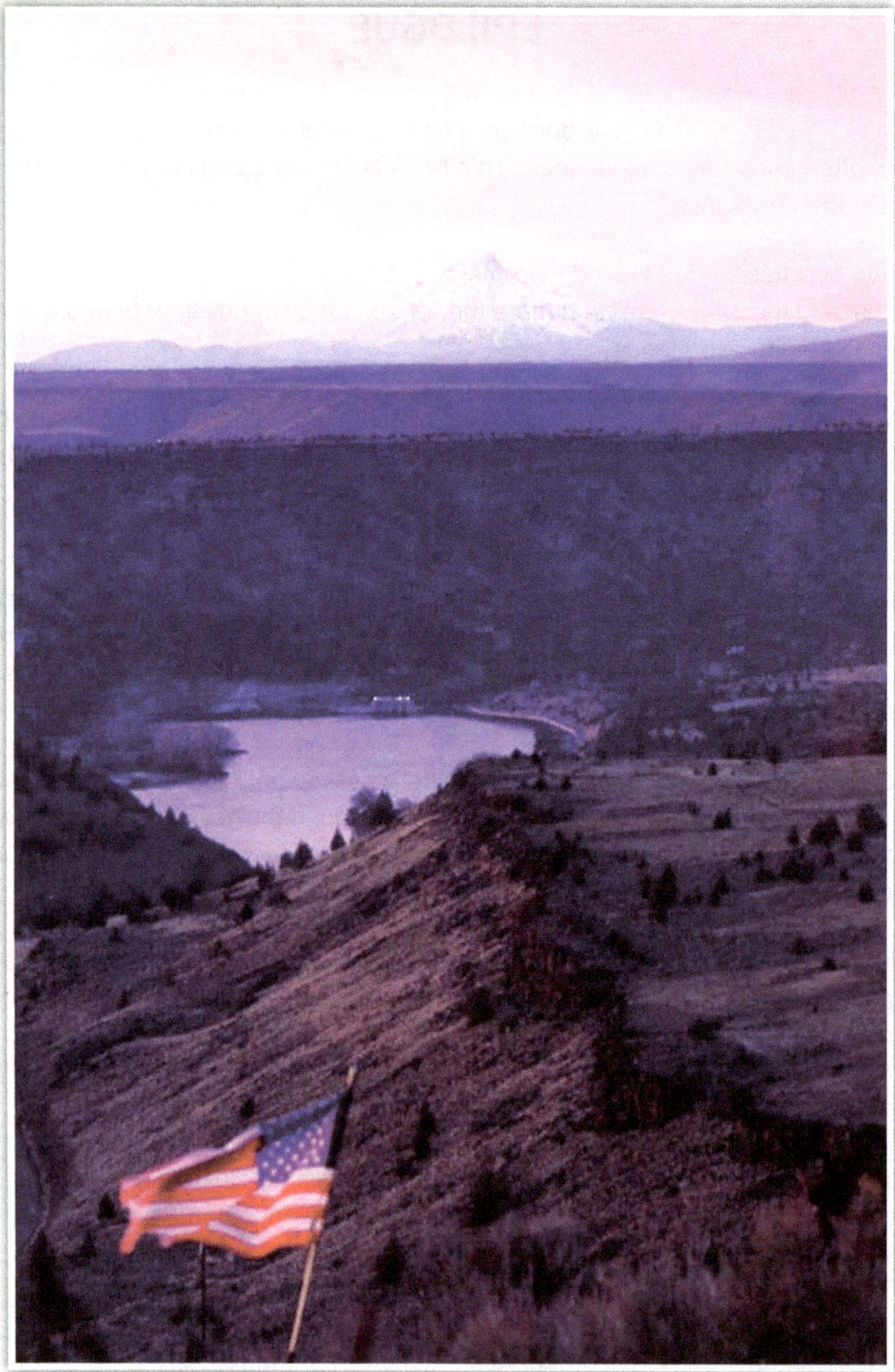

With Old Glory in the foreground and Mt. Hood in the background, the Deschutes River leaves its last impoundment at Warm Springs and begins its glorious one hundred mile journey north to the Columbia River. Author.

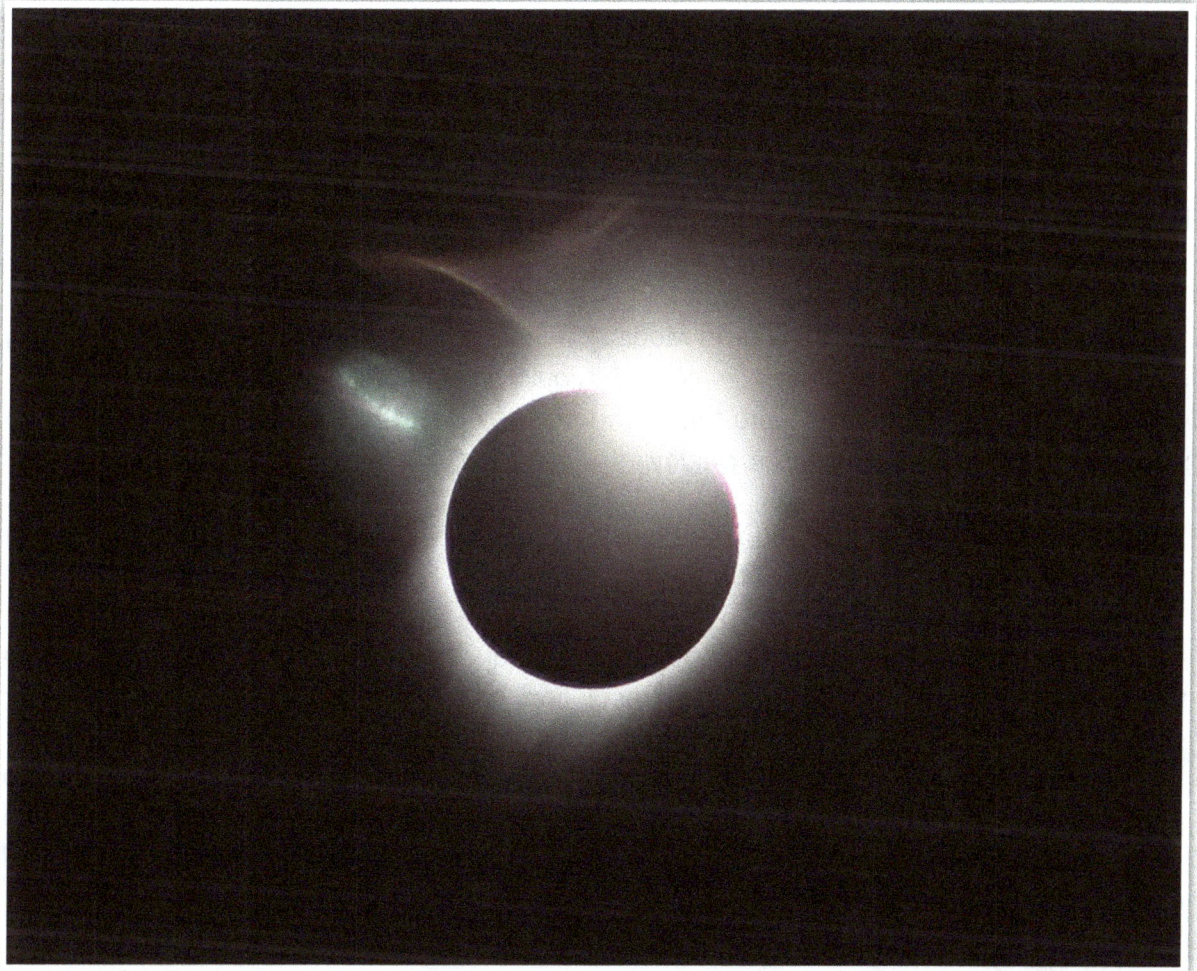

Total Solar Eclipse: Mother Nature's ultimate expression with the "diamond ring" that binds us to protect her. Bud Beamer, Rainshadow Ranch, Madras, Oregon August 21, 2017.

ACKNOWLEDGEMENTS

ONE IS ALWAYS UNCERTAIN WHETHER his or her efforts are worthy enough to share with others. I did have several individuals review the manuscript and received enough encouragement to move forward.

I asked former English professor and friend Jarold Ramsey, professor and writer Ted Leeson, and fishing writer and photographer Jim Schollmeyer to review the rough draft and provide advice. Jim was helpful with not only his suggestions, but also in sharing several of his professional photos for which I am grateful. Hernan Jordan, who manages Redsides Lodge, has always been supportive and truly a soul-mate.

David V. Evans, a former medical partner, who is now an associate professor of family medicine at University of Washington Medical School, was also most generous in sharing several photos from his archives. I wish that I could have had Jim or David with me on my outings so that their cameras were taking the pictures instead of me with my iPhone. I do apologize for some of my pictures' quality.

Bruce Bischof, a long- time friend, has been supportive and charitable in sharing several of his exquisite photos from his popular work.

I am also appreciative of the work done at the 1 Hour Photo Shop in Madras and the time they spent making the photos the proper resolution.

I am always indebted to my family for their patience and understanding when I have been so preoccupied with my profession, the book, and my semi- futile efforts to be a hay farmer and cattle rancher. Beth Ann, Annie, Jennie, Jordan, and Abigail are always there for me and, of course, Todd is always with me.

ABOUT THE AUTHOR

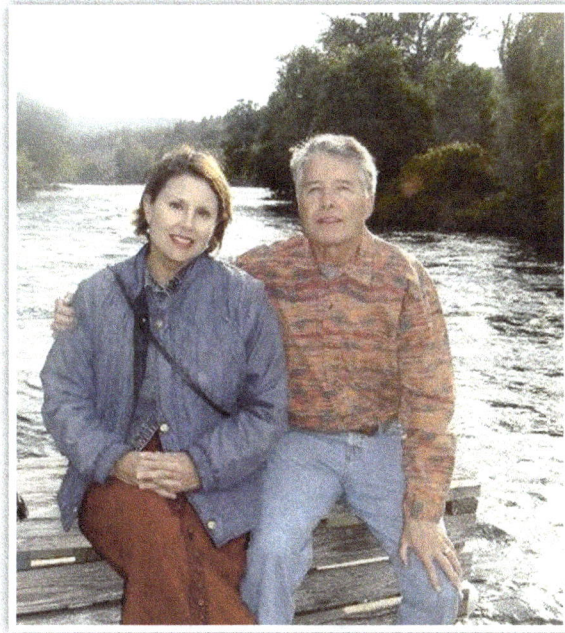

*Bud and Beth Ann enjoying the moving water
near their cabin on the Deschutes River.*

Leland "Bud" Beamer was raised in Iowa and attended Cornell College and the University of Iowa School of Medicine. After his internship in Portland, Oregon, he spent two years as the sole physician on the Warm Springs Indian Reservation in Central Oregon. The Deschutes River forms the forty mile eastern border of the Reservation.

After a family practice residency and surgical training, he was a family doctor, surgeon and ER physician in Madras, Oregon, for 40 years. He is currently chief medical officer at Deer Ridge Correctional Institution in Madras.

He still has roots in Iowa, but his love of Central Oregon and all of the natural settings and outdoor activities have provided a marvelous balance of recreational and professional activities.

Issues involving the early childhood period are of utmost importance to him. His book "the Baby and the Seed" is an illustrative work on the importance of love and nurturing in this critical period.

www.ingramcontent.com/pod-product-compliance
Lightning Source LLC
Chambersburg PA
CBHW080421030426
42335CB00020B/2540